THE CATHEDRALS

THE CATHEDRALS OF ENGLAND

ALEC CLIFTON-TAYLOR

Photographs by Martin Hürlimann and others
with 203 illustrations, 4 in colour,
26 plans and a map

THAMES AND HUDSON
LONDON

REPRINTED 1969

500 18070 9 CLOTHBOUND

500 20062 9 PAPERBOUND

PRINTED IN GREAT BRITAIN BY JARROLD AND SONS LTD NORWICH

Contents

To all those friends with whom, through the years, I have shared the delights of cathedral visits

Foreword

THE CATHEDRALS OF ENGLAND have for many years been one of my special loves; they have been the object of repeated visits; by now my conclusions about them are fairly definite. So the publishers' invitation to provide the text for the reissue of some of Dr Martin Hürlimann's splendid photographs in a book of lighter weight and more convenient size, and at a price which should make it accessible to a wider readership, proved irresistible.

Dr Hürlimann's original photographs were published seventeen years ago with notes by Dr Peter Meyer. Those in the present edition are, however, more comprehensive, and I gratefully record that where it proved impossible for Dr Hürlimann to fill the gaps, no objection was raised either by him or the publishers to my obtaining additional photographs from other sources. Here the National Monuments Record was of the greatest assistance.

Among the numerous books devoted to this subject are a good many that are more authoritative than mine; many are also far longer, and their authors could therefore enter into much greater detail. This is a comparatively short book in which it has been necessary to be selective. While there are certain historic milestones, like William of Sens's choir at Canterbury, which no writer on this theme could omit, my aim has been to concentrate primarily upon what I feel to be the outstanding excellences of English cathedral architecture and decoration, analysing, often by comparisons, their particular qualities and frequently adding aesthetic judgments that must, I am aware, be largely subjective. Perhaps in the arts a subjective approach is more defensible than elsewhere.

At the end of the book will be found short summaries written primarily for those not yet familiar with the cathedrals of England; their intention is to indicate which buildings are best worth seeing and what are some of the most memorable features of each. Some readers may therefore like to turn to those pages first.

CHAPTER ONE

The Master-works of English Architecture

UNTIL the time of Queen Victoria the cathedrals were easily the largest buildings in England, if by size we mean area of space enclosed. A Blenheim or a Wentworth Woodhouse might occupy a greater acreage, but would be subdivided internally by innumerable partition walls. Not until the development of iron and glass for building purposes were Englishmen to see still vaster spatial envelopes, structures such as the Crystal Palace and the splendid arched train-shed of London's St Pancras Station, the cathedral of the Railway Age.

They were the largest buildings, and they were also the greatest. They still are. The mediaeval cathedrals are the supreme expression of English architecture.

Two hundred years ago, a judgment such as that would have been greeted with derision. Here is the view of Tobias Smollett in *Humphry Clinker* (1770):

> The external appearance of an old cathedral cannot be but displeasing to the eye of every man who has any idea of propriety and proportion, even though he may be ignorant of architecture as a science; the long slender spire puts one in mind of a criminal impaled, with a sharp stake rising up through his shoulder. These towers or steeples . . . may be of use for making observations and signals; but I would vote for their being quite distinct from the body of the church, because they serve only to make the pile more barbarous or Saracenical.

About the same time, we find the architect Batty Langley observing that

> Gothic was a crude and unmethodical order of architecture which resembled neither Doric nor Corinthian, whose columns were sometimes two diameters high and sometimes twenty, and might be, as far as rules were concerned, two hundred.

1 WINCHESTER: The north transept
(an engraving of 1817 from Britton's *Cathedral Antiquities*)

That is interesting, because it reveals one of the reasons why the Georgians had such a low opinion of Gothic: it obeyed no rules. There was no predetermined relationship between, for instance, the diameter of a pier and its height.

Nowadays it would be generally agreed that one of the most enjoyable characteristics of the cathedrals is their unending variety: despite affinities of detail, no two are really much alike. In the eighteenth century, this was a ground for particular reproach. Batty Langley continues:

> All sorts of foliage were used in the capitals. The cornice profiles were eternally varying. And, worse than all, those ignorant Goths . . . directly violated the most obvious principles of eurythmia.

Hence the characteristically Georgian title of one of Langley's books: *Gothic Architecture Improved by Rules and Proportions*. . . . Even Horace Walpole, writing to his friend Sir Horace Mann in Florence, contrasts the 'true taste' of Italian Renaissance architecture with the 'venerable barbarism' of the Gothic North.

In the seventeenth century Classical principles had not yet taken so firm a root. At Oxford and Cambridge, during the first half of the century, Gothic was still blooming like an October rose, and as late as 1668 Wren himself was praising Salisbury Cathedral not only for its chaste lancet-windows and its reticent ornamentation but also for its proportions – both of nave to aisles and of height to width in the nave itself. Others, however, were far less sympathetic. Even in 1624 Sir Henry Wotton, in his *Elements of Architecture*, had expressed his opinion of Gothic:

> This form, both for the natural imbecility of the sharp angle itself, and likewise for its very Uncomelinesse, ought to bee exiled from judicious eyes, and left to its first inventors, the Gothes or Lombards, amongst other Reliques of that barbarous age.

(However strongly one may disagree with the sentiments, there can be no two opinions about the grace and charm of the writing.) Later came John Evelyn, an unrelenting critic. He found Lord Arlington's rebuilding of the church at Euston in Suffolk in the 1660s 'most laudable, for most of the Houses of God in this country resemble rather stables and thatched cottages than temples in which to serve the Most High'. And an entry in his diary runs thus:

> Greek and Roman architecture answered all the perfections required in a faultless and accomplished building. The Goths demolished these, and introduced in their stead a certain fantastical and licentious manner of building: congestions of heavy, dark, melancholy, monkish piles, without any just proportion, use or beauty.

Fantasy, licence, no rules, no canons of proportion: that was what, in the Gothic, worried the Classical school so much. In another passage Evelyn refers to the piers of the Gothic churches, the kind of design which can be seen to perfection at, for example, Wells, as 'Bundles of Staves and other incongruous Props'! *Ill. 47*

Such views were, it need hardly be said, by no means confined to England. Here is just one quotation from abroad. Of Jakob van Campen, the architect of the Mauritshuis at The Hague and, in 1648, of the Town Hall at Amsterdam, both strictly Classical buildings, it was said that 'he vanquished flowing Gothic folly with Roman stateliness, and drove old heresy forth before an older truth'. So there it is again: the folly and heresy of Gothic, and above all its denial of *truth*. There have been times when men of sensibility have felt very strongly about this, and these times may recur. For underlying it is the old, familiar antithesis between Classics and Romantics. In the eyes of the Classic, truth in architecture is identified with perfection. The Classical architects of the seventeenth and eighteenth centuries believed that the Ancients, by a process of infinite trial and error, had been able to evolve specific rules for the attainment of perfection. To throw all these overboard, to drown them without trace: that was the Gothic heresy. The Romantic was not, however, interested in abstract ideas of perfection. The design of every new building no doubt represented a new challenge, but a challenge, maybe, of a more pragmatic kind.

On such terms it might be supposed that Gothic cathedral architecture must be classified as Romantic. That would in fact be a misleading over-simplification. The unceasing experimentation of mediaeval church architecture, not only in England but all over Western Europe, is certainly one of its most striking characteristics and greatest sources of fascination; but to assume that the architects gave no thought to such matters as the balance between horizontal and vertical forces or the proper proportional relationship of the various parts would be entirely erroneous. The outstanding English example, Westminster Abbey, is not illustrated in this book since it was a cathedral only from 1540 to 1550; but there the designer was as concerned as any Classical architect with an abstract notion of perfection. The proportions of the internal elevation were determined mathematically: one-half of the total height for the main arcade, one-sixth for the tribune, one-third for the clerestory; 51 : 17 : 34=102 ft. Visually this is extremely satisfying.

More generally, it may be held that the length of many of the English cathedrals compared with their very moderate height led in time to the achievement of a delicate balance between horizontality and verticality. This was very different from, and less exciting than, the soaring aspiration of the great cathedrals of the Île-de-France, but closer to Classical ideals, into which excitement does not enter. Nor, on closer examination, are the cathedrals seen to depart far from one of the basic tenets of Classical architecture: symmetry. In this respect the Victorian architects, with their seemingly wilful but often deliberately contrived asymmetry, were far more Romantic than their mediaeval predecessors. Even the most prodigious creations of the final phase of cathedral Gothic, such as the pendant-vaults, were only achieved with the exercise of a brilliant and unassailable structural logic. That is to say, underlying the sense of wonder, which is Romantic, is the sense of order, which is Classical. The cathedrals stand not for any antithesis between Classics and Romantics but for a synthesis of the best ideas of each. I believe that here will be found some part at least of the secret of their enduring greatness.

Carlisle
Durham
Ripon
York
Manchester
Liverpool
Lincoln
Chester
Southwell
Lichfield
Peterborough
Norwich
Coventry
Worcester
Hereford
Ely
Gloucester
Oxford
St Albans
Rochester
Bristol
London
Wells
Guildford
Canterbury
Salisbury
Winchester
Exeter
Chichester
Truro

CHAPTER TWO

The General Aspect of England's Cathedrals

THE DISTINGUISHING mark of a cathedral is that it should contain the throne of a bishop. The derivation is from the Latin, and originally Greek, word *cathedra*, a chair, or throne. (This gave rise to the expression *ex cathedra*, meaning, literally, 'from the chair', hence by implication 'with authority'.) A cathedral is a building in which the principal man in the diocese, the bishop, has his chair of office. It need be neither large nor fine; abroad, in countries with many more cathedrals than England (Italy, for instance, has 275), a large number are architecturally insignificant. England has always favoured large dioceses, and not many of them; this made the cathedral, as the mother-church, a natural focus for legacies and endowments and other gifts, and so enabled it to grow both in size and splendour.

Apart from considerations of scale and decorative richness, the most obvious difference between a cathedral and an ordinary parish church is in the far greater development of the former east of the crossing. This was not only to provide accommodation for many more clergy but also, very often, to house the shrine of a saint, while in the middle Gothic period, when the cult of the Virgin became specially important, a Lady Chapel was added at the east end of a number of the cathedrals.

Although mostly dating from the Middle Ages, nearly all the Anglican cathedrals exhibit, within the compass of each single building, great divergencies of style. At the Reformation England had seventeen cathedrals, not one of which was in a single style throughout. London's St Paul's was later to be entirely rebuilt. Of the other sixteen, only three can show no Romanesque – or Norman, as this style of architecture is habitually termed in England: Salisbury, Wells and Lichfield. Sometimes the Norman portions will be clearly differentiated, as with the towers of Exeter or the nave of Southwell, and often they will form a substantial part of the whole

2 PETERBOROUGH: Interior, looking west

and will be recognized immediately. But even where they are less in evidence, the Gothic contributions may differ greatly in architectural character, as at Canterbury.

These stylistic variations, it must be admitted, have not usually worked out to the artistic advantage of England's cathedrals. Aesthetically the greater stylistic purity so often to be found in France is no doubt preferable. Yet such variations do add substantially to the interest of the visitor, who soon feels himself to be concerned with growing, almost living, organisms upon which many generations of men have left their mark, in contrast to the lovely but perhaps rather aloof perfection of a building such as St Ouen at Rouen, all completed in one style and hardly changed since. This continuing stylistic evolution, sometimes to be found in almost every phase within a single cathedral, means that throughout this book we shall be constantly returning to the same buildings.

Another, and very important, respect in which the English cathedrals differ from almost all those on the Continent is that some were united to monasteries. The bishop was also the titular abbot, but the effective head of the monastic establishment was the prior: hence these 'dual purpose' cathedrals were known as cathedral priories. The arrangement, an innovation of the Normans, often worked unhappily; the bishop was tactically at a disadvantage in his own church, and the prior and monks often jealous of their rights. The dual arrangement had notable effects on the planning, as will shortly be explained. Of the seventeen mediaeval foundations eight were monastic – or nine if we include Bath, which replaced Wells as the cathedral of Somerset between 1090 and 1218, when the joint diocese was set up. The other seven Benedictine establishments (besides Bath) were Winchester, Worcester, Canterbury, Rochester, Durham, Norwich and Ely.

The remaining cathedrals were served by canons, of whom there were two kinds in the Middle Ages, the Canons Regular and the Secular Canons. The former were so called because they lived in accordance with some fixed code (Latin, *regula*, a rule); and in England much the most important were the Augustinians or Austin Canons, whose rule of life was of a monastic kind, mainly deriving from the writings of St Augustine. They had only one church of cathedral rank, Carlisle, which was classed at the Dissolution of the Monasteries as a monastic foundation (hence the number, eight, mentioned above); two more of their churches, Bristol and Oxford, became cathedrals in the 1540s, after they had been ousted. Although the Austin Canons were by no means as rich as the Benedictines, at one time they owned over two hundred English abbeys and priories, and their more friendly manners and more liberal ideas made them less disliked than the monks unfortunately came to be.

The Secular Canons followed no set rule of life; and although responsible – as they still are – for the maintenance of cathedral services, they were free to live where they chose. Substantial funds were at times forthcoming from the sale of indulgences (the Church in fact had a vested interest in sin!); but the principal endowments were provided by income derived from the ownership of land – manors, and often churches too. These endowments were known as prebends (from the Latin *praebenda*, provender), and their holders were known as prebendaries. Membership of a chapter depended upon the possession of a prebend. Because of the Bishop's preoccupation with diocesan, and not infrequently in mediaeval times with political, affairs, the running of the non-monastic cathedrals devolved upon the Dean and Chapter, whose responsibility it still remains.

The cathedrals served by secular clergy, known since the time of Henry VIII as the cathedrals of the Old Foundation, are nine in number. In 1200 there were eight: five of pre-Conquest foundation, London, York, Lichfield, Hereford and Exeter, and three dating from the reign of William I, Lincoln, Chichester and Sarum. The following thirty years saw two changes, the last before the Dissolution: in 1218 Wells, another Saxon foundation, and a cathedral until 1090, regained from Bath its former dignity, and ten years later Old Sarum was replaced by New Sarum or Salisbury. It seems not unlikely that the rebuilding of the old church at Wells was the outcome of the determination of Bishops Reginald and Jocelin to escape from the domination of the monks of Bath.

Henry VIII, in the 1540s, created six more sees, of which

Augustinian Bristol and Oxford have already been mentioned. For his other four cathedrals great Benedictine abbey-churches were already available: Westminster (demoted again in 1550, after only ten years), Peterborough, Gloucester and Chester. No new sees were established between 1546 and 1836. Of the twenty new Anglican cathedrals created since then, eleven were conceived as parish churches, for which there is no space in a book of this compass, and four are new buildings. Only five, therefore, were venerable churches of mediaeval foundation, originally served by monks or canons. St Albans was a great Benedictine abbey; Southwark an Augustinian priory; Ripon, Southwell and Manchester were served by colleges of secular canons. Manchester, with its near-rectangular plan, looks un-cathedral-like, and has been so drastically rebuilt that it can no longer hold a place in England's 'vintage' set, which accordingly numbers twenty-six.

Except in Italy, where in some places the simple rectangle, with an apse at the east end, remained a favourite shape for churches right into the Gothic period, the larger churches all over Western Europe were, by the end of the eleventh century, nearly all being built on a cruciform plan. For this there were several reasons. The symbolism of the cross no doubt counted for much, the Latin cross plan conceived as the symbolic expression of Christ crucified. But there were at least two other factors. By 1000 the requirements of worship had become far more elaborate than in the days of the early Christians, and one of the needs was for more altars for the veneration of special saints. On the Continent this need was often met by the construction of lateral chapels between the buttresses of the nave; the altars might be on the eastern wall, or they might be placed facing north and south. In England the clergy were very insistent about orientation; they felt that it really mattered that the worshipper should face east. The advantage of a transept was that additional altars could be placed along its eastern wall, or chapels could be built out on the east side. The other explanation is structural. A massive central tower, which the English almost always favoured, demanded adequate abutment for the four corner piers: their outward-pressing

3 St Albans: Interior, looking east showing the nave altars and rood screen

thrust had to be counteracted in both directions. Thus, in addition to the walls of the nave and choir, the four transept walls running at right angles were also structurally essential. They could only be dispensed with where there was no central tower.

There was of course no structural need for the nave to be any longer than the transepts. So one naturally wants to know why, in England more than in any other country, the nave is often of immense length. The location of the proliferating secondary altars referred to above presented a problem, and one explanation of the long nave is that it enabled altars to be fitted in on the west sides of the piers. This can in fact still be seen at St Albans, where on the north side of the nave several altarpieces of the thirteenth and fourteenth centuries still survive. Also to be taken into account

Ills. 11–13, 160

Ill. 3

is the mediaeval practice of using the churches for many more purposes than is the case today. These included some which were secular or semi-secular, such as the administration of justice, the signing of agreements, the payment of tithe and so on. On the Continent such business appears to have been relegated wherever possible to an entrance vestibule (narthex) or a forecourt (atrium). But in England neither of these features is found. Large porches were built, and they were used for a variety of purposes: the English custom of posting up notices relating to local government in the church porch still survives as a reminder. A few of the cathedrals were provided with western transepts, and at Lincoln the thirteenth-century south-west transept is today the meeting-place of the Consistory Court, the court of the Chancellor of the diocese. During church festivals plays would be performed in the nave. In the Middle Ages, moreover, a church was often felt to be a suitable place in which to put the seal upon a commercial transaction, and the naves of large and important churches, some of the cathedrals among

4 SOUTHWELL: The pulpitum from the west

them, were undoubtedly put to such uses. In London after the Reformation the long nave of old St Paul's became the accepted place for a number of activities of scandalous irreverence.

The long naves of the English cathedrals are, however, best accounted for by recalling the dual purpose which some of them had to serve. Where both monks and laity had to be provided for, the church was in effect divided into two. The monks had the choir and the transepts, and sometimes, as at Norwich and in Westminster *Ill. 30* Abbey, the first two or three bays of the nave as well, in order to shut off the laity from the eastern of the two doors into the cloister. The latter were therefore confined to the nave, at or near the east end of which, in front of the rood screen, they had their own altar. Thus inevitably the nave grew longer.

It is not perhaps generally realized that these large cathedral-priories all at one time possessed both a rood screen and a pulpitum, and that their functions were entirely different. The rood screen was a development of the rood beam, and its purpose was to support the Great Rood or Crucifix, which, flanked by figures of the Virgin Mary and St John, was one of the most conspicuous objects of every mediaeval church interior. (Half a century ago a rood, unfortunately of no artistic merit, was re-erected at Wells.) The screen was pierced by two doorways, used for processions, to either side of the altar which was placed centrally against the western face. Most cathedral rood screens were of wood and have not survived; the usual situation, as at Norwich, was one bay west of the pulpitum. The only cathedral which still preserves its rood screen is St Albans; here it is of stone, *Ill. 3* and now supports an organ for which it was never intended. At St Albans it is the pulpitum that has vanished.

The pulpitum was also a transverse screen, but was devised for quite another purpose, with no specifically religious significance. The upper part of the rood screen, especially when of wood, was usually open, the apertures being filled only with unglazed tracery. But the pulpitum was solid – a massive erection several feet thick, nearly always of stone, pierced by a central opening with doors, as at Canterbury and York. The western side might also be pierced for altars, as originally at Exeter and perhaps at Southwell, but the *Ills. 109, 4* eastern side was always solid. The word signifies an elevated platform, and in that sense was the forerunner of today's pulpit. It frequently came to serve as a singing gallery and later, alas, to support the organ, so often a visually unwelcome intruder. But its primary purpose was to shut off the choir and to provide a backing for the return stalls, thereby securing for the monks or canons not only greater privacy but some protection from draughts, in buildings which, it should be remembered, were entirely unheated.

All the English cathedrals, whether monastic or secular, once had their pulpitum. (One was recently put back in its original position at Chichester.) Nothing is easier than to defend the pulpitum both on practical and on historical grounds. It is undoubtedly an aid to the conduct of services; and to sweep it away is to falsify history. But artistically the arguments for and against are much more evenly balanced. Ever since, in the middle of the twelfth century, Abbot Suger insisted upon opening up the interior of his bold new church at Saint Denis, this has always been a subject of controversy. It is significant that in the major French cathedrals there is now hardly a pulpitum to be seen (Albi is about the only important exception), and the aesthetic gain may well be felt to be considerable. But in England other considerations have to be taken into account. Vistas are now out of fashion; the professionals nearly always sneer at them. And aesthetically the solid screen can be an expressive 'punctuation mark'; but it can also cause frustration. In a very long church which is deficient in loftiness, like Exeter, or where there is an abrupt change of style between nave and choir, as at Gloucester and Canterbury, Rochester and Southwell, its artistic value is evident. Where these considerations do not apply, it may be felt that the pulpitum is aesthetically a more dubious asset. For a solid screen, with a large organ mounted aloft, works almost as effectively as an iconostasis in the churches of the Greek Orthodox faith in severing the eastern arm of the building from the rest. I am not one
Ills. 2, 13 of those who feel any sense of deprivation at Peterborough; where there is loftiness and stylistic unity there is nobility in the grand sweep. One certainly would not now advocate the removal of any mediaeval pulpitum that has survived, excellent though it would

often be to shift to another position the organ which now encumbers it. But I can think of no lost pulpitum which I would like to see replaced. So often people tend to stress the view east and forget that the view west may be still finer. At Rheims there is just a light open screen of cast iron, which looks very well. Wrought iron is still better: the early Georgian screen at Derby is a delight.

Much the most attractive solution to the problem of providing places for secondary altars was to throw out a series of small absidal chapels, not only from the east side of the transepts but also from the semicircular ambulatory or processional path surrounding, at a lower level, the main apse of the church. This arrangement was developed far more boldly on the Continent than in England. It can be specially well seen in the Île de France, where it is known as the *chevet*, meaning, literally, 'the head of the bed'. Five chapels was the usual number for a large church, but Amiens and Beauvais each have seven, ringing the apse. In England, unfortunately, a reversion was made in the early Gothic period to the flat east end of Saxon days; Westminster Abbey has the only Gothic *chevet*, and even this is not complete, as the middle one of the five chapels was later destroyed to make way for the entrance to that of Henry VII. Nor even in the Norman period was the flat east end entirely abandoned, but to this phase belong the only three examples of cathedral *chevets* which have even partly survived: Norwich, Peterborough and Gloucester. These will be described in the next chapter. Several theories have been advanced to account for the English abandonment of this noble architectural form; probably it was because of the need, in a northern clime, for better light at the High Altar.

So, in England, W.H. Auden's

> Cathedrals,
> Luxury liners laden with souls,
> Holding to the East their hulls of stone

are in fact less liner-like at the east end than elsewhere. Two main types are to be found. There is the cliff-like kind, mainly confined to the East and North, but occurring also at Worcester, Oxford and Bristol. The east end terminates abruptly, often in one immense

5 RIPON: The east end

Ills. 84, 163, 5 window, as at Lincoln, York, Ripon and Carlisle. In the other type
Ill. 6 there is a gradual falling away, in steps, as at Salisbury. This is the arrangement which, with variations, and in every instance as a result of later alterations, is also to be seen at Winchester, Chichester,
Ills. 115, 108, 155 Wells, Exeter, Gloucester, Hereford and St Albans, all cathedrals of the South or West.

A number of cathedrals of both types have the double transepts which make a striking contribution to the eastern development in England. These subsidiary eastern transepts, which were built at Cluny but seldom elsewhere on the Continent, certainly afford some consolation for the renunciation of the *chevet*. Their east walls afforded room for more altars. Places for still others were found in crypts, which sometimes also housed shrines.

On various other specifically English features there will be more to say in later chapters. But apart from the long naves and the flat

6 SALISBURY: The east end

east ends, the most distinctive characteristic of the English cathedrals is without doubt their skylines – their towers and spires. Here, ironically enough, the more modest scale of England's cathedrals as compared with those of France – their structural timidity, in fact – worked artistically to their advantage. Consider the height above the floor of some of the vaults. Wells (nave) only 67 ft; Lincoln 82 ft; Salisbury 84 ft; Westminster Abbey, with the loftiest mediaeval vault in England, 102 ft; Notre Dame, Paris, 110 ft; Chartres, 114 ft; Rheims, 125 ft; Amiens 140 ft; Beauvais 154 ft. Because of their audacious proportions, central towers for the cathedrals of the Île de France became a structural impossibility. All one finds are slender spires of wood covered with lead, as at Amiens; and sometimes not even that. In England, on the other hand, a central tower could always be built to scale without the need for internal piers so massive as to cause an obstruction. The central tower, sometimes surmounted

7 SALISBURY: View from Harnham Mill Pond

Ill. 7 by a spire, as above all at Salisbury, provides a focal point for the composition and a sense of balance which are profoundly satisfying, and comparatively rare on the Continent. Still finer are those English cathedrals with three towers, two at the west end and
Ill. 8 a larger one in the centre, of which Lincoln is one of the loveliest. The central tower here, 271 ft, is the second loftiest from the Middle Ages in England, and it once carried a timber spire believed to have soared to 524 ft, the tallest in Europe. Visible on a clear day even from the Wash, across forty miles of fens, this wonderful spire came down for ever in a great storm in 1548.

8 LINCOLN: A distant view by moonlight

CHAPTER THREE

The Norman Period

TO WRITE with any authority about English cathedral architecture in the eleventh and twelfth centuries is very difficult. To begin with, the survivals are haphazard. Owing to fires, to faulty building methods, to changing needs, or perhaps just to an enterprising churchman wanting to replace an old building by one that would be better lit and more up to date and, as he felt, more beautiful, the major part of the cathedral architecture of this period, and of the carved and painted decoration, has vanished for ever. This includes whole churches, like Old St Paul's, London. Moreover, the outlines of much of the surviving evidence have been blurred by later accretions, modifications and restorations. The documentation, largely in Latin, is also extremely incomplete and may be in libraries as far away as Copenhagen, Rome or New York. One can hardly hope, therefore, to achieve more than a fragmentary stylistic picture. It is like attempting a jigsaw puzzle with over half the pieces missing.

Romanesque, the style of art which preceded the Gothic, flourished all over Western and Central Europe. In England it falls into two phases, the Anglo-Saxon and the Norman; and in every branch of art except architecture, the Norman Conquest actually resulted, for a while at least, in a decline from the achievements of the Anglo-Saxon period. When the Normans settled in England, the country had been Christian for a little over four hundred years. The artistic survivals from those four centuries include some of the finest illuminated manuscripts ever produced in England, some exquisite embroidery, and a certain amount of remarkable sculpture. But as builders the Anglo-Saxons do not seem to have been very skilful, and only one minor example of their architecture can be seen in any of the English cathedrals. This is the crypt at Ripon.

Of their larger undertakings – among them the church at Ripon which stood over the crypt, the minster at York, and above all the

9 ST ALBANS: The crossing and north transept

great church which Bishop Aethelwold built in the second half of the tenth century when Winchester was the capital of England – we know all too little. Only of their last large church, Edward the Confessor's Abbey of Westminster, are we accorded, from the Bayeux Tapestry, a tantalizing glimpse. This church was almost certainly the first in England to emulate the Romanesque style of Normandy. The tapestry shows the death of Edward and his body being carried in state to the abbey. There are a round-arched arcade, clerestory windows and a lofty central tower with corner-turrets. The plan appears to resemble that of Jumièges, the most famous Benedictine abbey in Normandy.

The Normans were the greatest builders of their time, not only in Normandy and England but in Apulia and Sicily too. From this later phase of Romanesque architecture in England there are still magnificent survivals; but subsequently not one escaped substantial alterations. Seldom are these changes and additions any cause for regret; until the beginning of the sixteenth century, at any rate, those who altered the churches nearly always improved them. The buildings became much lighter, the decoration richer, and the masonry immeasurably better. But these changes made in the Gothic period do render it less easy to obtain an accurate picture of what a Norman cathedral really looked like.

To see the oldest example, we must go to St Albans: one of the largest, but not one of the finest, of the English cathedral churches. Yet despite architectural crudities, and specially harsh treatment in the Victorian period, this is still, internally, a building of austere majesty. The exterior is less enjoyable, but of interest for being the only mediaeval cathedral in the country not to have been constructed of dressed limestone or sandstone. St Albans is in Hertfordshire, a county very poorly supplied with natural stone apart from flint. So flint it had to be: nodules of silica, intensely hard but mostly small and quite amorphous; for a great church, an unpropitious material indeed. For the angles of a wall, a door or a window, unbroken flints were impossible. Nor was brick-making practised in England at this time. Nevertheless, the builders had a good supply of bricks on which to draw, for at the bottom of the hill, hardly a mile away, were the ruins of the Roman town of Verulamium. The thin, tile-like bricks of the Romans proved invaluable, and play at least as large a part as the flints in the external picture. *Pl. II*

There had been a Benedictine abbey on this site since 793, founded to commemorate the first British martyr, St Alban, a Roman soldier who had been beheaded here nearly five hundred years before, during the persecutions under Diocletian. The church was entirely rebuilt between 1077 and 1115 by Paul de Caen and Richard d'Aubeney, the first two Norman abbots, and from 1154 until 1396 St Albans was the premier abbey of England. At the Dissolution of the Monasteries, however, it lost its status and its glory; it was fortunate to escape destruction. It became a parish church, the largest indeed in England, and much too large for the town it had to serve. It accordingly fell into a very bad state of dilapidation, from which it was rescued (1877–1894) by a single, very rich man, who was unfortunately his own architect. Although raised to cathedral rank in 1877, this did not help, for the Bishop granted Sir Edmund Beckett (later Lord Grimthorpe) a faculty which in effect gave him a completely free hand. The big, ugly circular window in the north transept is one of his legacies.

Despite this deplorable window, the view across the transepts *Ill. 9* affords the best impression of the appearance of Abbot Paul's church. For its date, the scale was certainly bold. The absence of all sculptural enrichment can no doubt be attributed to the material; the huge brick piers were plastered over, whitewashed and adorned with a series of simple geometrical patterns, but of carving there is none. The only shafts are the short, bulgy ones in the triforium, probably a relic of the earlier, Saxon church; but the cushion capitals which surmount them are characteristically Norman. Nowhere was any vault attempted. Each transept had a pair of apse-ended chapels along its eastern side, but these have all disappeared.

Norman work of the Conqueror's time can still be seen in one other English cathedral: Winchester. Only the transepts preserve *Ill. 1* their original character. Built in 1079–1093 of limestone brought from the Isle of Wight, these are altogether superior to the pair at St Albans. The kind of proportion which was chosen in 1062 for the

Abbaye aux Hommes at Caen recurs in a number of major English churches: the distinguishing feature is the large gallery above the aisles, often referred to as the 'triforium gallery' but better termed the tribune. Some may feel that these large upper galleries, dark and cavernous, have an archaic character; they were in fact abandoned before the end of the thirteenth century, one of the last examples being in Westminster Abbey. Yet aesthetically there is much to be said for these dark openings, especially when, as at Winchester, they frame subsidiary arches. As one's eye travels up the wall there is a satisfying alternation of light, dark, light.

Designing in the Romanesque style continued in England until very near the end of the twelfth century. There is accordingly a full century to consider: a century, moreover, of intense building activity. Who can fail to respect the faith and courage of men who, faced with continual disasters from fire and inadequate knowledge of building techniques, would start anew, undaunted? Architecturally, within certain limits, there was a good deal of variety. To try to cover everything here would be impossible; nor, in a book primarily concerned with stylistic changes and aesthetic appeal, need we be bound too strictly by chronology.

The proper method of appraising a mediaeval cathedral is to go straight in, because its design, like that of most modern buildings and in direct contrast to the Greek temples and to Renaissance and Classical buildings generally, was certainly conceived from the inside outwards. This is not to imply that the exterior was left to take care of itself – far from it; but the primary uses of these cathedrals were internal. What was asked of the builders was to enclose space in such a way that the requirements of the Christian ritual could be met. This might be done boldly but crudely, as at St Albans, or with the utmost subtlety, as was to be achieved later. One of the particular joys of visiting the cathedrals is to discover how many experiments were made in every direction, in an attempt to reach the perfect solution.

In examining the Norman interiors, five factors will be found to be of major aesthetic importance: the relative proportions of the three stages – main arcade, tribune and clerestory; the shape of the

10 CHICHESTER:
The nave, looking west

piers; the employment, or not, of engaged shafts and of string-courses to provide vertical and horizontal articulation for the successive bays and stages; the method of dealing with the arch of the tribune; and the solution adopted for the ceiling.

At Chichester, as might be expected, the design owed a good deal to Winchester. The nave here was begun in 1114, although the present ashlar facing and the vault were only introduced after a fire in 1187. But the general proportions – rather low arcade, massive multiform piers, vertical engaged shafts and twin arches under the main arches of the tribune – all recall Winchester. *Ill. 10*

11 NORWICH: Interior, looking east

12 ELY: Interior, looking east

At Norwich, where work started at the east end, as was the usual practice, the nave was reached about 1120. In the fifteenth century the original wooden ceiling made way for the present magnificent
Ill. 11 vault. Otherwise the original fabric survives intact, except only for some of the windows, which were also replaced during the Gothic period. String-courses are present here but are kept subsidiary to the vertical shafts, which play a very important part aesthetically in giving definition to the successive bays. The tribune openings, particularly large in this instance, contain no subsidiary arches and as a result are somewhat cavernous.

The naves of the two other cathedrals of eastern England, Ely and Peterborough, are fine examples of the Romanesque style, despite the fact that unfortunately neither was vaulted. At Ely the nave probably dates from between about 1110 and 1130. Like Norwich
Ill. 12 it is very long, and the impression of height is enhanced by its comparative narrowness. Later alterations to the windows have ensured ample light, although in its abundance of wretched Victorian glass no cathedral is quite so unlucky as Ely. Nor can it be denied that one feels a certain incongruity at the sight of such massive walls, such strong arches and such an array of shafts supporting nothing more than a timber roof. But the ordonnance is immensely impressive. In its proportions, 6 : 5 : 4 for arcade, tribune and clerestory, it attains a maturity not hitherto encountered; and at the middle stage the openings, as at Winchester, are subdivided. Moreover the horizontal articulation, by means of string-courses, is now hardly less emphatic than the vertical. The creamy white Barnack limestone is a material fully worthy of so fine a design.

Peterborough, also built of Barnack stone (indeed, this monastery owned the quarries), has preserved its original Norman fabric internally to an exceptional degree. It is the latest in date of the three, and the richest: some of the principal arches have the billet moulding; at the tribune stage the chevron adorns not only the arch mouldings but the surface of some of the tympana which they
Ill. 13 encompass; and below the windows the blank walls are everywhere made interesting by means of an arcade which, following the example of Durham, is intersecting in nave and choir. As at Norwich

13 PETERBOROUGH: Interior, looking east

14 PETERBOROUGH:
South aisle of the nave, looking east

and Ely the aisles are stone-vaulted, but whereas those vaults were
Ill. 14 only groined, here there are ribs; and clumsy as they are, these massive ribs convey a sensation of masculine vigour. But except for a single bay at the west end, all the high ceilings are again only of wood; as at Ely the engaged shafts sweep right up, yet in neither building is there any evidence that a vault was intended.

As for the design of the piers, this was clearly a time for experiments. In these three great cathedrals of eastern England several forms can be found, not all equally pleasing. Some have multiple shafts and others are without; but always an engaged shaft will be seen, stretching up from floor to ceiling between each bay. Thus was achieved, in the eastern counties, the all-important factor of vertical articulation, aesthetically so necessary in order to counter the strongly horizontal 'pull' produced by these very long and rather narrow naves.

Elsewhere, and notably in the West, the Norman interiors strike quite a different note. At Hereford, despite the introduction of rather unconvincing pairs of engaged shafts, it is the large cylindrical piers that are dominant. (They are not in fact quite circular, measuring in diameter about 7 ft 2 in. from W. to E. and 6 ft 8 in. from S. to N.) In Romanesque architecture the cylindrical pier may be considered as something of an English speciality, for it is far more common in England than on the Continent. It can without doubt be very imposing, but it suffers from two disadvantages. The transition from the plain surface of the pier to the mouldings of the arch is awkward. This is inevitable; as the view of Gloucester shows still more clearly, the two forms are mutually incompatible. The one does not lead into the other, and the interpolation of a capital can do little to remedy this formal dissonance. Vertical shafts present an equally insuperable problem. It has already been shown how aesthetically necessary they are. But if a truly circular effect is the aim, as at Gloucester, obviously no engaged shaft can be tolerated; if such shafts are introduced, as they were at Hereford, it is only a change for the worse.

Ill. 15

Ill. 16

15 HEREFORD: The nave, looking west

16 Gloucester:
Interior, looking east

Of the upper parts of the Hereford nave this is not the place to speak, for the single west tower collapsed in 1786, and in the subsequent reconstruction James Wyatt removed the Norman tribune and introduced a quite different design of his own. Before that disaster the twin shafts continued upwards to support, originally, a wooden tie-beam roof. Today the abrupt break in the vertical shafting is very unfortunate. The nave of Gloucester is far more impressive, in spite of considerable aesthetic deficiencies. No rules of proportion such as were imposed on the Greek column were applied to the circular piers of Romanesque architecture. The length and the diameter could be varied at will. In the choir aisles at Gloucester the piers are decidedly squat. In the nave, on the other hand, it may well be felt that, at 31 ft, they are uncomfortably tall. Certainly the rest of the elevation is quite disproportionate. There is no tribune here – which is unusual in a large Norman building – and the triforium is but a midget. Unluckily, too, the point of springing of the thirteenth-century vault is much too low, so that horizontally there is no continuity at all at the level of the clerestory.

Nevertheless, with all its defects, it is difficult to enter the nave at Gloucester without experiencing a sensation almost of awe. Its design would seem to have been derived from Tewkesbury, an equally impressive building, surpassed only by Westminster Abbey and Beverley Minster among England's non-cathedral churches. These very lofty cylindrical piers, of great size (not comparatively slender, as at Tournus), are a good example of one of those local developments in Romanesque architecture which occurred all over Western Europe during the eleventh and twelfth centuries. They were a feature of the naves of at least four Benedictine abbey churches in the West of England: Evesham and Pershore in Worcestershire, both long ago destroyed, Tewkesbury and Gloucester in Gloucestershire. Piers of this proportion occur nowhere else.

With the Cathedral of Durham we reach the incomparable masterpiece of Romanesque architecture not only in England but anywhere. The moment of entering provides an architectural experience never to be forgotten: one of the greatest that England has to offer. Internally, moreover, the preservation of the original

Norman building is unusually complete. The design is quite unlike any other. The arcade is lofty – two and a half times that of the tribune – yet not excessively so. The dark shadows of the tribune arches emphasize the subdivisions which characterize all the best designs. The piers are of two types, circular and composite, employed in regular alternation. And, greatest difference of all, Durham was stone-vaulted from the outset. Begun in 1093, the whole church, except for the towers, was completed in only forty years, with every part vaulted. It was a prodigious achievement. *Ill. 18*

The vault of the choir, erected about 1100, was very bold for its date, but developed cracks and had to be replaced in the thirteenth century. The transepts were vaulted some ten years later, and these are the earliest high-level ribbed vaults in Europe. The function of the ribs which, like everything else at Durham, are very massive, was both structural and decorative; they strengthen the vault and also provide a pleasing finish. Then came the nave, and with it at the vault, another great innovation: the transverse arches, for the first time, were pointed. This was aesthetically a great advance, for it was now possible to obtain a level ridge without depressing the diagonal ribs, as had been done in the transepts. But whereas the quadripartite vault, with the ribs forming a simple St Andrew's cross, occurs over every bay, the transverse arches are only introduced where there is a composite pier – that is, between each alternate bay. This produces quite different rhythmic sensations from the feeling of regular progression which characterizes Ely, Peterborough and Gloucester. *Ill. 17*

Even here the point of springing of the vault is unfortunately too low – the one major criticism which can be passed on this design. Otherwise the proportions are wholly admirable: the relationships of height to width, of mass to void, of plain to ornamental surfaces – all seem exactly right. Moreover, the structure was completely sound. By the time he reached the nave, the Durham architect, probably earlier than any other in Europe, had fully mastered the problems of abutment involved in the erection of a high vault. To many it comes as a great surprise to learn that the Durham nave has flying buttresses. They are not visible outside, for they are concealed by the sloping roofs of the tribunes. Nor do they play nearly so

17 DURHAM: The nave, looking west

important a part as do the buttresses in fully developed Gothic, because at Durham the vault structure is more rigid and its weight is largely taken by the huge sandstone piers. There seems no doubt, however, of their value in helping to check what was always one of the special dangers of the high vault, the tendency of the clerestory walls to bulge outwards.

18 DURHAM: Interior, looking east

Both in its use of flying buttresses and of pointed arches, the first sign of that flexibility at the vault which was to become such a splendid feature of Gothic architecture, Durham was a harbinger of the new style. Yet in its immense massiveness, slow, solemn rhythms and pervading spirit, to say nothing of its ornamentation, this cathedral is still wholly Romanesque.

Ills. 20, 21 The composite piers are fine, and the engaged shafts sweep up without interruption. The circular piers, as elsewhere, make no concession to the form of the moulded arches, and the transition as usual is somewhat awkward. But the richness and variety of their geometrical ornamentation go far to compensate for this. Often in Romanesque churches the decoration was merely painted on, but here it was incised, after the construction of the pier was complete, with unforgettable audacity. There are four motifs: the diaper, the *Ill. 18* chevron, the vertical flute (executed, needless to say, in a more rough-and-ready fashion than in Greek architecture but none the less very effective) and, in the choir and transepts only, the spiral. These deep channels may once have been filled with metal, but if so there is no need to lament its disappearance, for the hollows introduce shadows in which there is much virtue. The chief ornamental motif, however, is the chevron, which enjoyed great popularity in England throughout the twelfth century. It adorns many of the vault ribs and mouldings in all parts of the building. It is seen in the interlaced arcade, admirably bold in scale, which runs all round the walls of the church, and again in the chapter-house and in the Galilee *Ill. 22* chapel, where it was employed to produce a cumulative effect of considerable if also somewhat barbaric-looking richness. In France

19 *left*. DURHAM: Bronze 'Sanctuary' knocker

20 *above right*. DURHAM: North aisle, looking east

21 *above far right*. DURHAM: East side of the north transept

22 *right*. DURHAM: The Galilee chapel

the Galilee (see Glossary) could be a vestibule as wide as the church itself; at Ely and at Lincoln it was a large projecting porch, but at Durham it served as a Lady Chapel. This very unusual – indeed, unique – position for a Lady Chapel, at the west end of the church, is always attributed to St Cuthbert's abhorrence of women. Whenever, the story goes, they tried to build the chapel in the usual position at the east end, behind the high altar, the Durham saint miraculously intervened to cause the foundations to cave in. So here it is: a low building at the west end, which at the end of the eighteenth century Wyatt was only just prevented from destroying, in order to carry a drive across the west front.

As has been indicated, it is no longer easy to be sure how most of these great Norman churches looked from outside when they were first completed. The views of Durham must always have been spectacular by reason of its extraordinary site, bestraddling a lofty tongue of rock round which the River Wear describes an elongated
Pl. I horseshoe. Specially famous is the view from the south-west, with the low Galilee chapel in the foreground, perched on the edge of a
Ill. 64 wooded precipice; of the three towers only the lower parts of the west pair are Romanesque.

It would be a pity to leave this glorious building without pausing
Ill. 19 a moment to look at the bronze 'Sanctuary' knocker on the north door. Apart from the disappearance of the coloured enamel which once filled the eye-sockets, and which need not be in the least regretted, this superb piece of Romanesque metalwork has survived intact. The stylization, especially of the hair, is beyond praise.

The cathedral whose west end best preserves its original Romanesque aspect is Southwell. This comparatively small building, in Nottinghamshire, off the main arteries of road and rail traffic, is perhaps the least known of all the English cathedrals. Undeservedly so, however, for Southwell harbours some choice delights, to which
Ill. 23 we shall return. The west front was completed about 1140. The window was inserted later; what sort of windows these Norman fronts originally had is not known for certain, but it is likely that there were several tiers of small single lights. The short pyramidal

PLATE I DURHAM: View from the south-west

spires, rather reminiscent of Germany, are a nineteenth-century reconstruction, but probably follow the original arrangement, for there were hardly any tall spires in Europe before the thirteenth century. The Southwell front is certainly plain and, it must be admitted, excessively flat, but it has a kind of gawky, homespun quality which is not unlikeable.

Another type of Norman façade is represented by the much-restored west front of Rochester. The interest here centres on the turrets, the two outer ones (both rebuilt) not a symmetrical pair. Their surfaces are all embellished by blind arcading, some of which is interlaced and profusely ornamented. Later alterations embrace not only the large window but the low pitch of the embattled gable. *Ill. 24*

Far more ambitious is the west front of Ely. Incomplete as unhappily it is, this is without doubt the finest of the Norman façades. It is also the most unusual. For Ely had a second pair of transepts at the west end, and a single west tower rising between them, providing a terminal feature for the nave. Such an arrangement was of continental derivation and in Britain occurs now only here and in the much-ruined abbey at Kelso in Roxburghshire; formerly it could have been seen at Bury St Edmunds, and may have been planned, at least, at Norwich. The original front at Ely, most of which belonged to the Late Norman period and the years immediately following, underwent later modification in three important respects. In the thirteenth century a large two-storeyed Galilee porch was added in front of the tower. In the fourteenth century the tower was completed by the addition of an ingenious but not wholly appropriate octagon flanked by four tall octagonal turrets; until 1801 this tower carried a lofty lead-covered wooden spire. And in the fifteenth century – probably: unfortunately there is no documentation – the north-west transept collapsed. It was never rebuilt; aesthetically this is a great loss. But what remains is still imposing, and the treatment of the wall surfaces offers a dazzling display of Late Norman exuberance. Never was the English love of blind arcading indulged to better advantage. The many variations in the form and scale of the arcades, to say nothing of the variety of the decorative enrichments, ensure that interest is not for a moment lost. *Ill. 25*

PLATE II ST ALBANS: The central tower

23 SOUTHWELL: Viev
from the north-west

24 ROCHESTER: Viev
from the south-west

25 *right*. ELY:
The west front

The impact of almost every Norman elevation depends upon a multiplicity of small effects, varied vertically but repeated in regular sequence horizontally. Partly, no doubt, this was because the art of constructing windows with stone tracery had still to be learned. *Ill. 26* Hence one almost always finds, as at Norwich, that the original design has been to a greater or less degree compromised by the insertion of larger windows, usually during the fourteenth or fifteenth centuries, to improve the internal lighting.

Norman towers fell like ninepins. The collapse could lead to a magnificent sequel, as at Ely, or to an architectural disaster, as at Hereford. Of the few that survive, much the most ambitious is at *Ill. 27* Norwich. Completed about 1145, this is the tallest Romanesque

26 NORWICH: South side of the nave seen from the cloisters

27 NORWICH: The nave, transept and tower, from the south-west

tower in England. But unfortunately in 1362 during a storm the lofty wooden spire was blown down on to the roof of the presbytery, and brought down part of the tower with it. Thus, whereas the original design is preserved, the stonework has had to be extensively renewed. The tower is very well proportioned, with angle-turrets covered with shafts bundled like reeds, to emphasize their verticality; but its surface ornamentation, although elaborate, has none of the rich exuberance of the Ely façade. With its stiff patterns of arcades, circles and lozenges, it would seem to have been designed by a mathematician rather than an artist. It looks best, therefore, from a little way off, whence its scale, and that of the fine stone spire added about 1490, impart great distinction to the building.

28 EXETER: The south tower

Ills. 28, 108 Exeter is no longer a Norman cathedral, but has kept from the earlier building its massive pair of towers, which were built over the transepts. Towers in this position are very unusual, but occur occasionally on the Continent (although never in Normandy); in England the cathedral of Old Sarum also had them, and about 1260 the church at Ottery St Mary in Devon was to follow suit. Aesthetically, towers so situated are not very satisfactory, although at Exeter, as presently we shall see, they made possible an effect of great splendour. The arcades have zigzag decoration, but the motifs are as severely geometrical as at Norwich, and less resourceful. Like many Norman towers, they were originally crowned with squat pyramidal spires. The late-fifteenth-century pinnacles and battlements may be considered an improvement.

Ill. 29 Earlier than any of these are the towers, built about 1115, which adjoin the west sides of the eastern transepts at Canterbury. Too small ever to be seen as a pair, these are none the less survivors of considerable charm, depending once again upon an aggregation of small effects for their adornment.

29 CANTERBURY: The south-east transept tower

As was said earlier, only three Norman *chevets* are even partially preserved. At Gloucester the apse itself has gone, as has the apsidal chapel beyond it, which was replaced in the fifteenth century by the present spacious Lady Chapel. But to left and right of this Lady Chapel a pair of Norman chapels still survives, each two storeys high – indeed, three, if the crypt is included. Peterborough has lost all its chapels, but has kept its apse, much marred as it is by the insertion of Decorated windows with strangely inappropriate tracery under ugly segmental heads. Internally, although the loftiness of the apse is pleasing, the omission of a stone vault even here is not very easy to accept. So again the palm goes to Norwich. Here, in contrast to Peterborough, it is the lower stages which are mainly Norman; after the spire fell the whole eastern arm was given a much loftier clerestory, with tall traceried windows and flying buttresses to counteract the thrust of the superb stone vault added near the end of the fifteenth century. At ground-level today's central chapel is a modern replacement, but otherwise the Norman arrangement survives unaltered. The north-east and south-east chapels, consisting *Ill. 30*

30 NORWICH: The presbytery

on plan of segments of two overlapping circles of differing diameters, are, it must be admitted, more curious than beautiful. On the other hand, the continuation round the apse not only of the ambulatory but also of the tribune above it produces a fine three-dimensional effect of great strength. The later Gothic windows and vault blend astonishingly well with the Norman work below, and despite the widely divergent dates the presbytery of Norwich is among the most beautiful in England.

On the subject of sculptural decoration, there is not a great deal to be said. The Norman cathedrals display plenty of decoration of the semi-geometrical type (especially the chevron), but architectural figure sculpture, in England as in Normandy, was introduced sparsely. Capitals were mostly based on variations of the plain cushion form; other details, such as corbels, are much more interesting at some of the village churches, where the old Anglo-Saxon traditions continued. This even applies to the relief carvings in the tympana, the spaces between the lintels and the arches of the doorways. Remote village churches, especially in Herefordshire and Gloucestershire, can show some very spirited examples of these, but in the cathedrals they are decidedly scarce.

The nearest English approach to the great sculptured doorways of the French Romanesque churches is the west door at Rochester, *Ill. 31* but it is certainly modest by comparison. The exuberantly carved voussoirs, recalling the churches of Aquitaine, date from about 1160. Some fifteen years later were added the sculpture in the tympanum and the two figures attached to the second pair of columns. The tympanum has a Christ in Majesty. He is seated within a vesica, with a standing angel on each side and the Four Beasts symbolizing the Evangelists. On the lintel are the Twelve Apostles seated as judges. The two figures below, recalling those on the west front of Chartres, represent Solomon and the Queen of Sheba. Considering the high quality of all this sculpture, it is very unlucky that it is not better preserved. It may possibly have been the work of a Frenchman, coming from the region of Poitiers.

31 ROCHESTER: Sculpture above the west door

32 *above*. ELY: The Prior's door   33 *right*. ELY: The Monks' door

Moving northwards, French influence lessens. At Ely the Norman cloisters have gone, but three doorways which formerly gave access to them from the church have survived. On the cloister side two of
Ill. 33 these were elaborately sculptured. That known as the Monks' door has mainly ornamental motifs, and no tympanum; the other, called
Ill. 32 the Prior's door and dating perhaps from 1140, has much more figure carving, including another Christ in Majesty supported by angels in extremely contorted poses, and medallions on the jambs containing dancers, musicians, birds and a variety of curious grotesques. These doorways are not great art. Although the hollows are fairly deep, the surfaces are flat and rely for their effect upon complicated linear elaboration. The figure of Christ is stiff and lifeless. Yet for all its limitations this sculpture does possess a certain semi-barbaric splendour, seen especially in the pair of heads on the Prior's door which, as corbels, support the lintel. Their big bulging eyes transfix us.

34 *left*. LINCOLN: Detail of the central west door

35 *below*. LINCOLN: Romanesque relief above the south-west door. Left to right: Noah building the Ark, Daniel in the lions' den, the Ark coming to land

36 *right*. LINCOLN: The west front

At Lincoln the Norman cathedral was so badly shaken by an earth tremor in 1185 that everything had to be taken down and rebuilt except the west end, and this was later much altered. Archi- *Ill. 36* tecturally the west front is now a hotch-potch, but the central part still incorporates considerable remains of an important scheme of decorative sculpture, carried out shortly after a fire in 1141. This embraces three doorways and a long frieze set into the wall above and beyond them. Unfortunately the stone of the doorway carvings decayed, and had they not been extensively recut in the last century some of them would have been lost for ever. Only the frame of the central portal has figure carving, but here it is abundant. The close view of the upper left-hand side of this doorway shows men and beasts amid trailing foliage, while the innermost column has a *Ill. 34* succession of beak-head masks, a pre-Conquest ornamental motif which became a favourite with the Normans. The scalloped capitals are adorned with pellets, cables and scrolled foliage. The survival at Lincoln of part of a large seated figure of Christ points to the existence in the twelfth century of a tympanum of considerable size over this doorway. The frieze is also sadly incomplete; the whole of the important central section was replaced as early as the fourteenth century, and there are other gaps. In the part reproduced, the *Ill. 35* scene within the frame, showing Daniel in the den of lions, has no obvious connection with the rest, which tells the story of Noah. The only other Romanesque church which has a frieze at all comparable to this one is the cathedral of Modena, which Bishop Alexander of Lincoln probably saw in 1145 on his way to Rome, and from which there seems every likelihood that he borrowed the idea. In these stocky little figures and informal groups there is a geniality which is not often found in English sculpture at this time.

For in truth this was not a genial age. As a rule, in looking at Norman figurative art, we find ourselves asking what can be the significance of all these strange, pagan-looking fantasies, often so ebullient, sometimes so grotesque, now and again so cruel. Some of the sources of this repertory of images are known: the herbals, the astronomical and medical treatises, the fables attributed in the Middle Ages to Aesop, and above all the bestiaries. Others are rooted in the

37 CANTERBURY: The crypt

everyday experience of the time: the Labours of the Months, for instance, and the hunting scenes. But others again can only be accounted for by reference to the social conditions of the period, which were by our standards appalling. 'The snapping jaws are never far behind men's heels', T.S.R. Boase writes, in a memorable passage;[1] 'puny man creeps about with his axe under over-shadowing beasts: frail, naked humanity is for ever caught in the coils. They are the images of an age hardened to unalleviated pain, to the wearing pangs of undiagnosed disease and its no less agonizing attempted cures, to wounds and blows, to the arrow that flieth by day and the pestilence that walketh in darkness.' Hell, in fact, was often on

38–39 CANTERBURY: Capitals from the crypt

earth; no wonder, therefore, that it figured so frequently in the art.

Such thoughts are not wholly absent when confronted, in the
Ill. 37 crypt at Canterbury, with a series of capitals that include some of the finest examples of Norman architectural sculpture in England. The choir at Canterbury is raised so much above the nave that the crypt, with windows later enlarged, is much better lit than most. The structure was complete by 1107, but the capitals were carved later *in situ*, which was not of course the usual mediaeval practice; and some were never carved at all. The four faces of each capital were treated independently, as is perfectly feasible with capitals of the cushion form. They are in at least three different styles and vary a good deal in quality. But among them are about fifteen that reach a really high artistic level, and two or three which are masterly. These appear to date from the 1120s. The subjects are mostly drawn from the realm of fable: curious animals and fantastic monsters in conflict furnish some of the best themes, and they would seem, in some cases
Ill. 38 at least, to be of Eastern origin. On one a strange bird is attacking a serpent, probably a symbol of evil. Near by there is a capital with
Ill. 39 another splendid struggle-scene, this time between a dog and a wonderful flying dragon with human arms that grab at a big foliate tail. It is a richly animated composition, a work of marvellous accomplishment, for any date.

40–41 CANTERBURY: Capitals from the crypt

Away to the right of the crypt, in the chapel of St Gabriel,[2] are two more remarkably fine examples – two faces of the same capital. One has a dancing, faun-like creature, a kind of satyr, seizing the muzzles of two shaggy-coated wolves with long, improbable tails. An excellent convention has been evolved for the representation in stone of rough wool. Both the subject itself, and especially the symmetrical arrangement of the wolves, point again to an Oriental derivation. Best known of any are the music-making beasts. Fantastic animals engaged in music were always a favourite theme of Romanesque fancy. To the left a winged creature, part ram, part woman, is playing a rebeck, an early kind of fiddle. Facing him, playing a recorder, is a no less lively goat, with again a foliate tail. The goat is perched upon a dragon, but uneasily, for the dragon is biting his forearm. The rendering could hardly be more spirited; and, although the sources of these designs were undoubtedly illuminated manuscripts, it is remarkable in what completely sculptural terms the different textures – feathers, skin, wool and so on – are represented. Very satisfying also is the manner in which all these compositions have been adapted to the cushion-capital form. They combine qualities found together nowhere else in the sculpture of the Norman cathedrals: vivid imagination, a splendid decorative sense and considerable technical mastery.

Ill. 40

Ill. 41

CHAPTER FOUR

The Earliest Cathedral Gothic

ENGLAND'S FIRST truly Gothic buildings belong to the last thirty years of the twelfth century. They were not, of course, labelled as Gothic, any more than their predecessors were described as Romanesque: the term Gothic did not make its appearance until the latter part of the seventeenth century, and then only with a derogatory signification. Nor was all English cathedral building at this time carried out in what is now called the Gothic style. At Peterborough, for example, the Benedictines, who usually tended to be conservative, were still building their nave and western transepts in a completely Romanesque idiom until 1193 – and in some discomfort too, from all accounts. In 1190 an abbot of Peterborough complained that forty windows in his church had been waiting twenty years for their glass and were still blocked with trusses of straw and reeds. England at this time, and for long after, did not make her own glass (except some of very poor quality) and glaziers were still scarce.

It was on September the 5th 1174 that the whole of the eastern part of the Cathedral of Canterbury was consumed by fire. About eleven years later one of the monks, Gervase, who was an eye-witness, wrote, in Latin, a detailed description of the fire and its aftermath. Although the original text does not survive, three copies do: one is in the British Museum and two are at Cambridge, and all three were written within the following century or so. Canterbury is therefore better documented at the time of the destruction and rebuilding of its eastern part than any other English church prior to Westminster Abbey. Gervase's account is of absorbing interest.

The fire had broken out by the church gate, the old Norman gate in Burgate Street which long ago disappeared. It enveloped three small houses. A south wind was blowing at the time 'with a fury almost beyond conception'; sparks and ashes, whirled aloft, landed on the church and became wedged between the lead roof covering

42 CANTERBURY: The Trinity chapel

and the wooden joists, which were already much decayed. Soon the sheets of lead began to melt, and the building suddenly burst into flames. Only the nave was saved.

> The grief and distress of the sons of the Church were so great that no one can conceive, relate or write them; but to relieve their miseries, they fixed the altar, such as it was, in the Nave of the church, where they howled, rather than sang, matins and vespers.[3]

Before long the brethren were discussing how best to repair the ruined church. It is not difficult to imagine some of the differences of opinion. Whenever a calamity causes a fine building to be destroyed, there are always those whose one idea is to rebuild it exactly as it was – and in certain cases this is undoubtedly the right course to follow. Often, however, it is not; if one has any faith in the architecture of one's own time, it should be shown by building in a contemporary mode. This is what happened in London after the burning of St Paul's in 1666; it is what occurred at Coventry – eventually, although the 1947 Commission, appointed by the Cathedral Council, recommended traditional English Gothic. It was also the decision at Canterbury. Initially, Gervase tells us, there were disagreements, which were only resolved when William of Sens, 'a man of great abilities, and a most curious workman in wood and stone', was appointed architect. He had been trained in his native France, at this time the most progressive country in Europe in the field of church building. Even to persuade the monks to allow him to take down the ruined choir was no easy task, and in fact, although the piers had to go, considerable portions of the outer walls were allowed to remain, as the visitor will at once observe. The pair of eastern transepts with their delightful little angle-towers, already described, the pairs of chapels flanking the former apse and the large crypt all belong to the pre-fire building.

The rebuilding occupied about ten years: 1175 to 1185. It is characteristic of the English cathedrals to extend a long way eastwards of the central tower: nowhere is this more strikingly in
Ill. 43 evidence than at Canterbury. Moreover the whole of this part of the

cathedral, miraculously escaping the German bombing in 1942, remains as an authentic and very little altered building of the last quarter of the twelfth century.

The plan is without parallel in England or in France. The short choir of Lanfranc's cathedral (1070–1077) – only two bays and an apse – had been extended under Anselm and Conrad in the early years of the twelfth century to embrace a pair of eastern transepts and the two chapels of St Anselm and St Andrew, placed obliquely against the former ambulatory. But even if there had been no fire, a further eastward extension would soon have been required to house the shrine of Thomas à Becket, who had been murdered in the cathedral in 1170 and canonized as St Thomas of Canterbury three years later. No other English saint was ever as popular. Pilgrims poured into the city. Buried first in the crypt, his body was carried upstairs in 1220 with much pomp and placed in a new shrine, the magnet which assured to Canterbury more than three centuries of abundant wealth. So magnificent indeed was Becket's shrine that Erasmus, who saw it in 1512, recorded that gold was the meanest thing to be seen there. Only twenty-six years later it was rifled and despoiled.

43 CANTERBURY: Air view from the south-east

The problem for the architects, William of Sens and his successor known as William the Englishman, was described in some detail by Gervase.

> The two towers [i.e. chapels, with crypts below] of St. Anselm and St. Andrew, formerly placed in a circle on each side of the church, prevented the breadth of the Choir from proceeding in a straight line. But it was judicious and useful to place the Chapel of St. Thomas at the head of the church, where was the Chapel of the Holy Trinity. The architect, therefore, not willing to lose these towers, but not able to remove them entirely, . . . yet preserving as much as possible the breadth of that passage which is without the Choir [i.e. the ambulatory] on account of the processions which were frequently to be made there, narrowed his work with a general obliquity, so as neatly to contract it over against the altar. . . .

And once past the chapels, the building swells out again slightly before the final contraction to the circular chapel known as the Corona, or Crown of Becket, in which was preserved a fragment of the saint's skull. The solution of the problem was ingenious, and the culminating feature, the Corona, is delightful; but to declare as some do that this unique plan endows Canterbury with a special subtlety is to claim too much merit for something which the architects would surely have been glad to avoid, had they been able to. The truth is that the eastern part of this cathedral is somewhat wasp-waisted.

After the stateliness and elegance of the two-centuries-later nave, many who pass into the choir must feel disappointed, particularly at first glance. Let it be said at once that the vault is at present dingy, and a thorough cleaning would no doubt work wonders, as the example of Westminster Abbey has demonstrated. Nevertheless this is a dry, angular design, of great interest as a pioneer work in the Gothic style, but of no great architectural beauty. The quality which
Ill. 45 is lacking is grace. The plain circular and octagonal piers, the Corinthianesque capitals, the nearly square abaci, the flattened form of the arch mouldings, the manner in which the engaged shafts below the vault ribs come to an abrupt halt on the abaci, and the

44 *left*. CANTERBURY: The north-east transept

45 *below*. CANTERBURY: The choir, looking east

sexpartite vaulting system – all these are characteristic of the earliest Gothic in France, and can be seen at Notre-Dame, Paris, which was begun in 1163.

Internally, lifted high above its crypt, the choir does not seem very lofty, but it was, Gervase tells us, much higher than the old one, and was vaulted throughout, where formerly there was only a painted wooden ceiling. The sexpartite vault is well seen in the view of the *Ill. 44* north-east transept. The unit is not one bay but two: the diagonal ribs, that is to say, rise only from every second pier. But from the intermediate piers a transverse rib climbs to a slight point and crosses the vault at its apex, thereby converting the vault unit from four compartments to six. Such an arrangement occurs in several of the Early Gothic cathedrals in France, but north of the Channel it is rare. The hollows of some of the ribs are enriched with a sharply cut moulding known as the dog-tooth, which for the next two generations was to achieve widespread popularity in England.

The walls of the east transepts were not rebuilt, but only heightened; the old Norman clerestory windows were embodied in a triforium (as distinct from the tribunes at this level in the choir). Another tier of purely ornamental arcading, with less sharply pointed arches, was introduced immediately below the new triforium. What characterizes all this arcading is the employment, for the first time in any quantity, of Purbeck marble for the shafts. This also was to set a fashion which was not followed in France but which was to have an immense impact upon the appearance of almost every large church erected in England for a full century hereafter. Thus there will be many references to this material in the pages that follow. It should, however, be observed forthwith that Purbeck is not a true marble. It is a shelly limestone, rich in fossils, and varies in colour according to the nature of the shells and to the range of impurities which it embodies. At Canterbury most of the Purbeck shafts are brown. Its attraction for the Early Gothic builders was that, alone among the materials which they had at their disposal, it would take a polish. A conglomeration of tiny petrified shells – and in Purbeck stone the predominant shells are those of the snail-like *paludina*, a freshwater mollusc – will yield, when polished, an

PLATE III CANTERBURY: Stained glass detail from the north aisle of the Trinity chapel

elaborate figuring which was highly esteemed. For external use this stone was of little value, as in the English climate the polish would not remain for long; and even internally it would soon look dull if the building were damp. But it was for its polish that it was called marble; and it would be pedantic not to use the term today, despite its inaccuracy. In support of the view that probably many cathedral interiors were damp, one may again turn to *Humphry Clinker*:

> When we consider our antient churches, . . . may we not term them so many magazines of rheums, created for the benefit of the medical faculty? And may we not safely aver that, in the winter especially (which in England may be said to engross eight months in the year), more bodies are lost than souls saved, by going to church?

If Purbeck marble was to be employed at all, its obvious use was for shafts, since it lies in very narrow strata, seldom above 1 ft in thickness and sometimes as little as 2 to 3 in. On the other hand it can be prised out in lengths of 6 to 8 ft. It was not the only English marble to be introduced into the cathedrals, but it was much the most important. Whether on balance these polished shafts, usually a good deal darker in tone than the rest of the masonry, were aesthetically an asset is a subject upon which opinions differ.

A striking feature of the long eastern limb of Canterbury is the continually rising levels. The choir is lifted – perhaps too much – above the nave; the presbytery is slightly higher than the choir; thence one mounts again to the Trinity Chapel and the Corona. It is a fine progression, contributing to the effect of a grand climax which was evidently required. The Trinity Chapel continues the design of *Ill. 42* the choir, with certain modifications: the arcades here are less lofty; the supporting piers, as at Sens, take the form of paired columns; the middle stage is a triforium, not a tribune. The beautiful Corona *Pl. IV* beyond contains the antique stone chair on which every archbishop sits at his installation.

In all this part of Canterbury Cathedral it is less the architecture than the stained glass that impresses. Not all of it is old, but the late- *Pl. III* twelfth- and early-thirteenth-century windows which survive are

PLATE IV CANTERBURY: The corona

beyond question the finest in England. York has more mediaeval glass than Canterbury, but the York windows are neither so ancient nor so fine. This is almost the only glass in England which in quality – not, alas, in quantity – is worthy to stand beside all but a few of the windows of Chartres (of which incidentally Becket's secretary, John of Salisbury, became the bishop). The twelve principal windows in the Trinity Chapel were devoted to the representation of various miracles alleged to have occurred through the intercessions of St Thomas. About half their original glass survives, and they are also notable for their wrought-iron armatures, another merit which they share with the best French windows. *Colour plate III* shows the lower half of the most easterly window on the north side, which has the finest armature of them all.

When the Cathedral of Wells was begun is not known for certain; it was not later than 1186 and it may have been ten years earlier, which carries us back to the time of William of Sens's work at Canterbury. Yet the two buildings could hardly be more different. Wells is – if we except the Cistercian Abbey of Roche, in Yorkshire – the first truly English Gothic church, a building that owes almost nothing to France.

The choir was considerably altered in the fourteenth century, and the earliest surviving portions of Wells are the transepts, the six eastern bays of the nave and the north porch, all of which were complete by 1215. This was the first mediaeval building in England in which the pointed arch was used throughout; no round-headed arches were employed anywhere. The view, on entering the nave, is
Ill. 46 inevitably dominated by the great strainer arches (see p. 164). But these were no part of the original design, nor of anyone's intention, and an effort should be made to 'think them away'. Compared with contemporary French cathedrals the size is small, and for a cathedral church even perhaps a little puny; from floor to vault, as has been observed, is only 67 ft. But although the scale is so modest, the proportions of this interior are excellent; and while we look in vain here for the spatial quality of the French churches or for comparable feats of planning (Wells was always square-ended: more so, indeed,

46 Wells:
The nave, looking east

originally than now), the surface enrichment, as so often in English mediaeval buildings, is a delight.

Where else in all England could one find more beautiful piers? *Ill. 47* The core of each pier is masked by slender shafts, arranged in eight groups of three: twenty-four in all. For these clustered piers the fine grey oolite from the quarries at Doulting, seven miles to the east of Wells, was an ideal material. Nothing equals limestone if one aims, as here, at composition in depth. The play of light and shade over the piers and over the equally complex arches affords unfailing pleasure.

48, 49 WELLS: Capitals in the south transept. Fruit stealers

The capitals and corbels also make a fine contribution. They are quite unlike the acanthus capitals in the choir at Canterbury, and far more vital. Nowhere can this English invention, the stiff-leaf capital, be seen to better advantage. The name is deliberately generalized, because it derives from no leaf known to nature; it is sometimes said to represent a combination of the acanthus and the vine, yet it does not closely resemble either. Even at Wells the stiff-leaf capitals and corbels vary as one moves from east to west, but nearly all of them convey a sense of sprouting vigour and are boldly undercut – which again means excellent light-and-shade contrasts. These staccato accents are beautifully in tune with the boldly broken surfaces of the massive piers.

In the transepts and the eastern bays of the nave many of the stiff-leaf capitals and corbels are enriched by the introduction of lively *Ill. 51* little heads, half-lengths, animals, grotesques and even narrative subjects, such as the story of the fruit-stealers. This well-known pier in the south transept displays four little scenes. In the first the thieves *Ill. 48* are seen at work. We sense the nervous way in which the one in the foreground is looking round to see whether anyone is coming. In the other scenes the owners sally forth and give chase. The thieves are apprehended. One is beaten with a pitchfork by the indignant *Ill. 49* owner, who holds him by the ear; the other receives a clout over the head. The carving is all very spirited. Another capital has a man with *Ill. 50* toothache, an almost obsessive subject (and not surprisingly) in an

47 WELLS: View in the Nave

Ill. 52 age without dentists. The lizard corbel in the east aisle of the north transept is deservedly famous. Both the lizard and the leaves are naturalistic enough to convey a sense of nature's energy; yet at the same time the form of the corbel is beautifully disciplined and was, we may suppose, conceived in the first place as an abstract shape. The carving of animal and foliage alike respects this shape, and is thereby a lovely decorative adjunct, as well as being so full of life. Vitality and good decoration are two facets of art which are often opposed, for vitality implies movement and good decoration is often static; but this corbel attains the ideal synthesis.

At Wells the perfection of the arcade, it must be admitted, is not carried through into the upper parts of the nave and transepts. In the transepts the bays are clearly delineated by vaulting shafts, even though they only rise from the base of the triforium; but in the nave, for some unaccountable reason, the division into bays was abandoned and the tribune hurries along in an unbroken line of small lancets. There is no vertical articulation in the middle register, and thereby the design suffers. The clerestory is very plain, and the vault has no ridge-rib. As a result, in the nave especially, there is little temptation to contemplate the upper regions; in marked contrast to the French cathedrals, the vertical 'pull' is weak. This horizontal emphasis is no doubt a recurrent characteristic of English Gothic, but at Wells it is felt to an exceptional degree.

The twenty-five years after 1215 were devoted to finishing the *Ill. 53* nave and building the major part of the great west front. For the completion of its towers this front had to wait nearly two hundred years. One can see at once what an ambitious composition it was, stretching out far beyond the aisles, to a total width of 147 ft. The initial reason for this was not architectural but doctrinal. The intention was that the façade should serve as a gigantic screen for the display of statuary; and so in fact it did. But it must first be considered as a work of architecture; and although it can be faulted on certain secondary points, and especially for the insignificance of the doors, this front is one of the masterpieces of English Gothic. West fronts designed as screens, several on an ambitious scale, can be seen at a number of other English cathedrals, but there is none which

50–52 *above*. WELLS: Capital from the south transept. A man with toothache. *below*. Corbel in the south transept. *right*. Corbel from the north transept aisle. A lizard

rivals Wells. The upper parts of the towers are, it is true, sometimes criticized for the omission of pinnacles; but it is arguable that this was done deliberately, in a design in which, as so often in English Gothic, the horizontal lines are at least as important as the vertical. The proportions are singularly harmonious. The great breadth of the front seems to be deliberately emphasized by the two strong horizontal string-courses which girdle it. Thereby it falls into three clearly defined horizontal zones, each with a distinct quality of its own. In the lowest stage, for example, the value of the plain base is at once evident, as is the strong effect of the boldly projecting gables of the lowest tier of arcades. But these horizontal divisions are admirably countered by the verticals of the six salient buttresses, which also serve, by their cast shadows, to add a third dimension and remove the effect of flatness which mars several of the other English fronts. The composition has a beautiful logic, and is quite unlike any other.

53 *overleaf*. WELLS: The west front ▶

The sculpture is also unique in England in respect of the quantity that survives. Originally there were three hundred and forty figures, of which about one hundred and fifty were life-size or larger. Of these three hundred and forty, there are today slightly more than half, some headless or mutilated in other ways. Some of the figures cannot now be identified, but the whole front presented one great theological scheme, illustrating the triumph of the Church. In the lowest zone, Prophets and Apostles: few of these remain. Then two rows of quatrefoils, with angels and Biblical scenes. In the middle
Ills. 55, 56 zone, martyrs, some of them martyred kings, and virgins to the left; confessors, in the guise of bishops and abbots, to the right, as on the south front at Chartres completed a few years before. Just below the upper string-course, the Resurrection of the Dead. In the stepped gable in the centre, angels, Apostles and a badly smashed Christ in Majesty. Although we can speak of a Wells style there were, needless to say, a number of sculptors, and the figures vary in treatment and in quality. But on all of them, thanks to the fine Doulting limestone, the draperies fall in graceful and often delicate folds. The tiers of sculpture are carried round three faces of the towers, and the north-
Ill. 54 west tower has even managed to keep several figures from the lowest range, tall austere persons who may be Evangelists, and on the east face young men who are believed to be deacons. By French standards, no doubt, all this sculpture is provincial; figure sculpture is not an art at which the English, through the centuries, can be said to have excelled, and, considered individually, many of these statues fall a good deal short of the highest standards. Yet as an ensemble, and notwithstanding all that it has suffered from puritanical iconoclasm and stone decay, the Wells front is still one of the great sights of England.[4]

A screen front of entirely different character, but after Wells the
Ill. 57 most remarkable, is Peterborough. It had been intended to finish off the nave with twin towers at the ends of the aisles, in a familiar Romanesque manner; one of these towers was actually built, and the other partly so. It was then decided to broaden the front by building out one bay to north and one to south, beyond the towers. Finished

54 WELLS: The north-west tower from the east

55, 56 WELLS: Statues from the west front

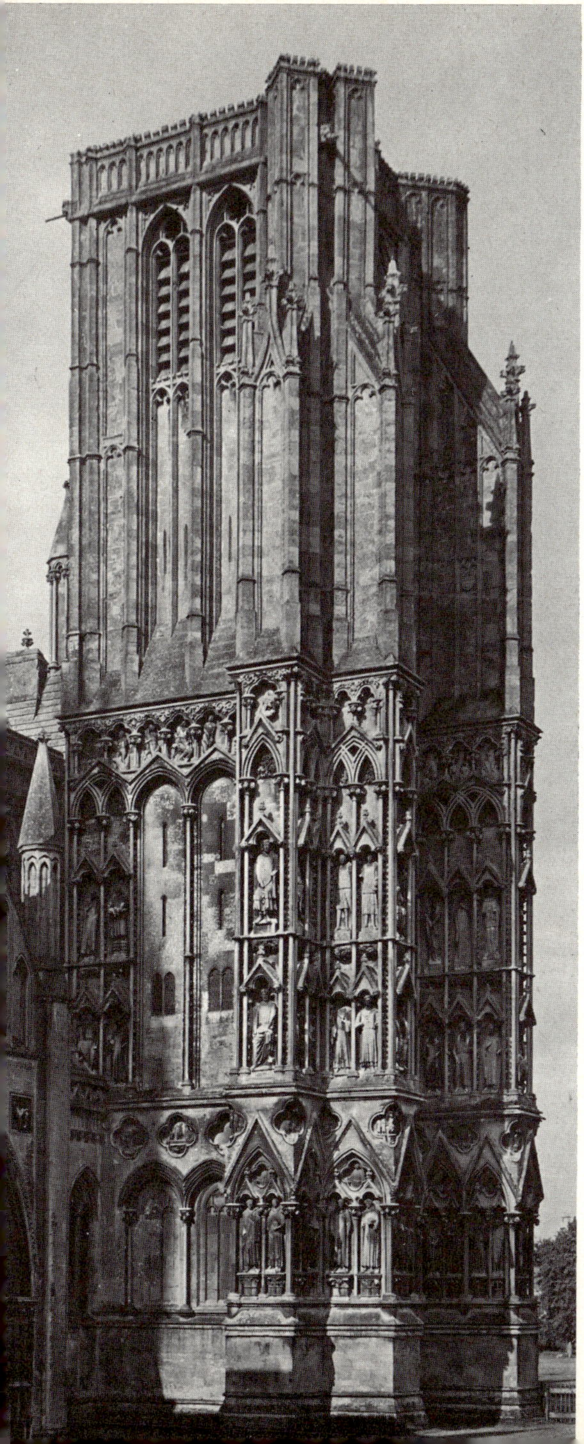

about 1190, these together constitute a small pair of western transepts. Then, scarcely a decade later and before the west front was finished, the whole design was scrapped and replaced by another of an entirely different character, in the nascent Gothic style. Why, and under what circumstances, remains a mystery.

This extraordinary front, one of the most dramatic conceptions in mediaeval architecture, is on a bigger scale even than Wells, with a width of 156 ft. The building dates are close, but the two designs have almost nothing in common. The sculpture here is much less important; there are only a few figures, of a rather squat, stocky type, and placed too high to be effective. The interest therefore centres almost wholly on the architecture, of which the precursor
Ill. 36 was certainly the original Norman west front of Lincoln, the core of the present façade. The dominant feature at Peterborough is the trio of huge arches, richly moulded, deeply recessed, and 81 ft high. They are not all the same size, as they would have been in Greece or Rome – or France: the central one is the smallest. It is not easy to say why this was done, for the three gables above, with their attractive rosettes, are very properly uniform both in height and in the angle of their slope, since the central one has a higher point of springing. The relative narrowness of the central arch is certainly no asset, but a pinched effect is avoided through the presence of the corner-towers, which stand even outside the ends of the west transepts. Although not massive, they are large enough to ensure that the vertical units here are not three but five: narrow, broad, narrow, broad, narrow. This adds considerably to the cathedral's appearance. The concept has a splendid audacity; and subtleties such as the variations in the intervals between the string-courses and between the annulets on the profusely moulded piers all point to the consummate artistry of the designer. Nevertheless, this front is not the equal of Wells, and this would be true even without the presence of two features which seriously disrupt its harmony. Except to note that they are not a pair, no regrets need be felt about the small spires added during the fourteenth century: that on the south tower is indeed a design of singular charm. But the large tower is another matter. A tower should never be left, as this one is, just peeping over

57 PETERBOROUGH: The west front

the top. Even if there were a pair, the effect would be far from good, but the presence of this one tower, off-centre, plays havoc with the skyline. The central porch is even more out of place. This was an addition of 1370, sometimes said to have been introduced to tie together the two lofty supports of an arch showing a tendency to 'spread'. If so, it was an ingenious solution, and the porch itself, with a chamber above which now houses the cathedral library, is not unattractive. None the less, its relationship with the façade is disastrous; the impact of the central arch is seriously compromised.

The weightiest criticism, however, does not depend upon extraneous factors, and it is fundamental. What is the relationship of this façade to the building of which it is, after all, the front? If we peer into the great arches we find that the doors opening into the aisles are tucked away in the corners: could any arrangement be more visually uncomfortable? And when the cathedral is seen from the side (and on approaching the city from the south the side view is dominant), it is all too evident that this tremendous front was just clamped on, with very little consideration for its relationship to the rest of the building. The Peterborough front was a *tour de force*, the Wells front an integral part of the building.

A recurring question among those who care about church architecture is: Which is the finest of England's cathedrals? The answer is not obvious. Clearly it partly depends upon the method of assessment. How do we measure fineness? In my view it is proper to take into account the accompaniments of architecture: architectural sculpture, carved ornament, stained glass, mural painting and woodcarving; but not tombs. I have never been able to make up my mind which one cathedral I consider the finest, but I feel able with some confidence to name the four finest: Durham, Lincoln, Wells and Canterbury. Yet all four suffer from substantial defects. So, as we visit and revisit each, we are not only delighted again by the beauties but shocked anew by the deficiencies. To this Lincoln is no exception. This marvellous building is at both ends, east and west, unsatisfactory. And internally, apart from a host of secondary criticisms that could be made, there is the basic question of the proportions.

58 LINCOLN: Air view from the south

As already observed, the Norman cathedral here was shattered, strange as it may seem, by an earthquake, a tremor severe enough to be felt almost throughout the country, on April the 15th 1185. Only the west front survived; the rest was so badly shaken that it had to be taken down to the ground. So, as a few years earlier at Canterbury, the chance was seized of building in its stead something more up to date. One of the particular beauties of Lincoln is that the scheme launched in 1192 under Bishop Hugh of Avalon was carried right through, with modifications only of details, to the completion of the Angel Choir in 1280. First came the choir and the eastern transepts, then the main transepts, to be followed immediately by the chapter-house, with its very prominent buttresses. The second quarter of the thirteenth century saw the building of the lower portion of the central tower, the nave, the west front as it now is, and the Galilee porch on the west side of the south-west transept. The only substantial later additions were the presbytery and retro-choir, always known here as the Angel Choir, the cloisters, the upper parts of the three towers and the now vanished spires.

Ill. 58 Both the aerial view and the plan tell us that Lincoln is, in sharp contrast to the French Gothic cathedrals, a building with a series of projections stepping out at right angles to the principal axis. The effect is not of concentration but, on the contrary, of diffusion. This is characteristic not only of Lincoln but of the English Gothic churches in general. It is on this point that continental, and especially French, criticism concentrates; and one understands why. With a shape like this, concentrated spatial effects in the French sense are impossible. Within, although they are of course related, we can hardly avoid looking at each part separately, in turn. And that was the way these great churches were built – section by section, as the requisite funds became available. Externally, such a shape as this means that the central tower becomes a feature of capital importance for giving unity to the design. Where the central featuie is missing, as at Westminster or Beverley, the appearance of the building suffers greatly. In all these Early Gothic buildings the central tower, and sometimes spire, were not finished until later, perhaps much later. Fortunately they nearly always were completed, for their aesthetic value cannot be overstressed. It is only upon entering these buildings that we become aware of the spatial limitations of English Gothic as compared with French.

Ill. 59 Lincoln's nave is on an altogether grander scale than that of Wells, and 15 ft higher; yet the vault is too low, and this defect is unfortunately accentuated by the fact that the piers are slender and rather widely spaced. Thus the proportions are not really satisfactory. At present the nave also has another drawback, which could be more easily remedied: the colour. The local limestone of which the cathedral is built is brownish yellow, and the Purbeck marble used in such profusion here is mostly very dark sage-green. With such a combination it would seem evident that, if the compartments of the vault are to be limewashed, they should be a brownish cream. Instead, they have been done in the coldest of whites, and the result is not happy.

Despite these necessary reservations, the interior of Lincoln offers a multitude of pleasures. Structurally the inspiration came from the choir of Canterbury, but in their total effect the two buildings are

59 LINCOLN: Interior, looking east

quite unalike. Where Canterbury is dry and devoid of charm – or would be, but for the gorgeous glass – Lincoln is characterized by a great wealth of carved and especially of linear elaboration. In no other English church was Purbeck marble, brought in ships from the quarries in Dorset which happened to be close to the shore, employed with such a lavish hand. The Purbeck marble shafts, eight to each pier, are free-standing, but are attached about half-way up by annulets or shaft-rings. The shafts could not be obtained in unlimited lengths, so the annulets also mask the joins between them. Some of the piers also have, recessed between their Purbeck colonnettes, eight more still thinner shafts.

Among the many other points at which Purbeck marble was introduced was the blind arcade beneath the lower windows. This charming feature, with trefoil arches carried on paired Purbeck colonnettes, was a typical Lincoln enrichment. The dark stone occurs again between the aisle windows; it is profusely employed for the elaborate arcade of the tribune, and supports another arcade in front of the clerestory windows. The handling of all this polychromy is carried through with unfailing assurance.

Above the main arcade, the nave of Lincoln is far in advance of Wells. There is vertical as well as horizontal articulation now, and a much finer vault. Over each bay there are not only diagonal and transverse ribs, the essentials of a quadripartite vault: there are also eight additional ribs, which have the same point of springing but which are not carried across from one side of the vault to the other in a continuous line. These are the tierceron ribs; and perversely enough, although the name is French, the form is peculiar to England. Since a pair of tiercerons always meets obliquely, it will be seen that a ridge-rib is essential. Lincoln has a finely moulded ridge-rib, with carved bosses covering every point of junction. The introduction of tierceron ribs is another example of that absorption with linear pattern which was always one of the distinguishing characteristics of Gothic architecture in England. The example of Lincoln nave was to be followed in a number of other cathedrals, and was to be responsible for several of the loveliest vaults ever built.

Earlier than the nave and the great transepts are St Hugh's choir

60 LINCOLN: Capital in the north choir aisle

and the east transepts. These, with their four eastward-projecting chapels, derive directly from Canterbury. With a vault eight feet lower than that of the nave, the proportions here are still more uneasy, and the design of the vault in St Hugh's choir is a curiosity which was fortunately never to be repeated; clearly, ribbed vaulting was still at the experimental stage. Where the architect excelled – and whether he was Geoffrey de Noiers or Richard the Mason is uncertain – was in his handling of detail. The stiff-leaf capitals and corbels are no less fine here than at Wells. The leaves break forth and *Ill. 60*

turn crisply back, and each one is deeply undercut. No individual leaf is represented, yet they have the growing quality, the bursting life
Ill. 61 of young leaves in spring. Arresting too is the blind arcading on two planes in the choir aisles. The figures in the spandrels have been restored, but the dark shafts of Alwalton marble,[5] the crisp stiff-leaf capitals, the boldly cut mouldings, some with dog-tooth, and the interlocking arches, all contribute to render this an exquisite piece of architectural decoration.

References have already been made to what Lincoln owed to Canterbury: in planning (later altered), in general proportions, in the design of the tribune stage, and especially in the abundant use of Purbeck marble. But there are other Canterbury features which do not appear at Lincoln: the acanthus-derived capitals, the square abaci, the flattened arch mouldings, the nearly round-headed windows, and, except in the transepts, the sexpartite vaulting; and these are exactly the features which Canterbury derived from France. Whether this was a coincidence or whether it was deliberate is impossible to say, but the outcome is plain: Lincoln, hardly less than Wells, is a cathedral which appears to owe very little to France.

When the building was completed, Lincoln could show a series of stained-glass windows hardly, if at all, less fine than Canterbury's. The loss of the greater part is therefore a tragedy. In 1644 the fanatical soldiers of the Earl of Manchester did appalling damage. About 1788 all the thirteenth-century glass that remained was collected from other parts of the building and placed where it now is, in the south transept and in the east windows of the choir aisles; the rose in the north transept never lost its glass, despite considerable mutilations. The glazier of 1788 sought to find for each body a head, for each head a body, with the result that a great deal more damage was done. Yet despite this sorry story the eight windows at Lincoln which still keep their early French-inspired glass are the most enjoyable in England after Canterbury, and provide a welcome contrast to the Victorian glass, of which Lincoln possesses a great deal. Enthusiasts for Victorian glass appear to hold this collection in high esteem, but the undeniable fact is that it produces darkness without richness.

61 LINCOLN: Wall arcading in the south choir aisle

An important feature of this cathedral, not only for its intrinsic beauty but also for its subsequent influence, is the polygonal chapter-house. Every cathedral had its chapter-house, which was the administrative office of the foundation. The earliest were rectangular, with the single exception of Worcester, which was originally circular (and is still so within) but has suffered from extensive reconstruction. *Ill. 62* Lincoln has the first of the polygonal chapter-houses, and set a beautiful fashion, peculiar to England. Most of these are octagonal, but this one is decagonal, with a diameter of 59 ft; it is therefore a spacious building. The original wooden roof was replaced about half a century later by a lovely star-vault fanning out from a central pier.

Ill. 63 The west front presents another large-scale example of the English preference at this time for a widely spreading screen, instead

63 *right.* LINCOLN: View from the west

62 *below.* LINCOLN: The chapter-house from the east

of the twin towers, one at the end of each aisle, which were still the rule in France. But unfortunately the Lincoln façade does not repeat the success of Wells, nor even of Peterborough. The Norman core, with its lofty arches which anticipated Peterborough, was retained, but nonsense was made of the central arch by giving it a new, pointed apex. Then, in the 1240s, above and to either side of this Norman core, was built a broad and lofty screen wall, adorned with tier upon tier of arcades, and culminating in a gable and a pair of octagonal angle-turrets. The result, although undeniably imposing, is not happy, and is very unkind to the towers, which are left to shoot up from behind in a most uneasy fashion. This screen has two tiers of small pedestals for figures and canopies for the lower row, but if any sculptures were added they have long ago vanished without trace. Its primary function seems to have been to provide, in the words of Peter Brieger,[6]

> a monumental stage set or scenic front for the triumphal entry of the processions, especially that of Palm Sunday, when the entry of Christ into Jerusalem was re-enacted year by year. The gigantic screen served the same function for the whole building as the screen inside for the choir.

Canterbury, Wells and Lincoln all had to wait a long time before their principal towers were carried up to their present heights. At Durham, on the other hand, as by 1200 the main architectural work was already accomplished, attention could be turned to the task of *Ill. 64* finishing the massive west towers. The entire surface of every upper face is covered with arcading, some still round-headed but mostly pointed, and nicely varied in scale and treatment. The towers gain greatly in effect from the areas of shadow produced by the piercing of many of the taller lancets. From probably the fourteenth to the mid seventeenth centuries these towers carried lead-covered wooden spires, which must have looked strangely out of harmony with the Norman building. The present pierced parapets and corner-pinnacles date only from about 1800. They make an excellent skyline.

64 DURHAM: The west towers, from the cloisters

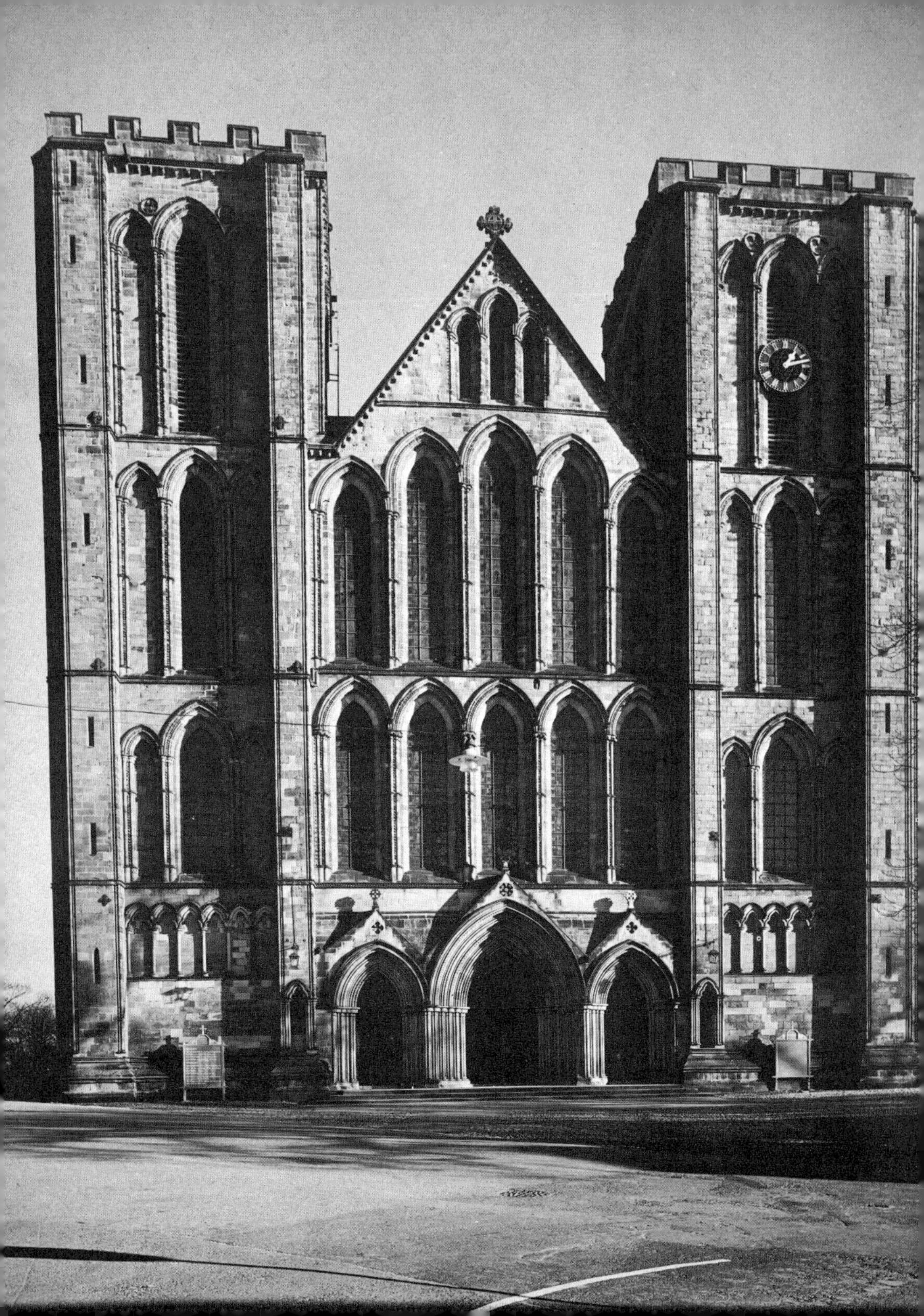

CHAPTER FIVE

The Maturity of Early English

IN LANDS long inhabited there are generally certain towns which in the course of time, for one reason or another, have shifted their sites and started entirely anew on virgin soil. Salisbury was such a town. Old Sarum, although little more than a mile away, is today only a barren windswept hill with nothing but large earthworks. Yet this was successively an Iron Age fort, a Roman settlement (Sorviodunum) and an early mediaeval town with cathedral, castle and houses. The Norman cathedral was small, but had, as was mentioned earlier, twin towers rising over the transepts, in anticipation of Exeter. Several reasons prompted the episcopal decision to abandon this building and move down into the valley of the Avon. There were the infertility of the soil, the coldness of such an exposed position and, in particular, a water-shortage. There was also a political factor: since the time of King Stephen the castle had belonged to the Crown, and the clergy and the royal garrison were on the worst of terms. It was decided, therefore, to descend to where there were water, fertility, a milder climate – and independence. Papal authority was finally forthcoming in 1219.

The Church was thus offered the opportunity of building a brand-new cathedral, and Salisbury's building history is less complicated than that of any other in England. The foundation-stone was laid in 1220, the Lady Chapel finished by 1225, the east transepts and choir by 1237, the great transepts, nave and beautiful north porch by 1258. Then followed the west front, cloisters and chapter-house. After 1284 there was a pause of fifty years before the launching of the tremendous project for the tower and spire, which was not finally completed until about 1380.

With the exception of London's St Paul's, therefore, no other cathedral in England presents so harmonious an architectural ensemble. The air view shows this beautifully. Did ever a building

65 RIPON: The west front

67 *right*. SALISBURY: View from the north-west

66 *below*. SALISBURY: Air view, from the north

compose better? Was there ever a more complete, a more delicious stylistic consistency? But one will be wise to concentrate on the ensemble. For in its details the exterior is nowhere near as rich nor as interesting as, say, Lincoln. Some features are not free from monotony: the continuous parapets, for example, supported on corbel-tables, also continuous, which incorporate no sculpture nor even a decorative moulding such as the dog-tooth. *Ill. 66* *Ill. 67* *Ill. 96*

The plan is lucidity itself. Except at the east end, the debt to Lincoln is obvious. The contrast between both of them and a typical French plan, such as Amiens, has often been made, and is instructive. The notable features of the Salisbury plan are the great length (473 ft) as compared with the modest width (at Amiens the length is only four times the width: at Salisbury it is six); the considerable projection of the transepts; the second pair of transepts, in the favourite English manner; the Lady Chapel (now the Trinity Chapel) at the east end; and the fact that every one of these projecting members is now straight-sided and right-angled.

As one moves inside, it is important not to forget what the designer was trying to do. He was aiming, above all, at achieving an appearance of lightness and elegance, in direct contrast to the heavy solidity of the Romanesque, which he had no doubt known at Old Sarum. There can be no question of his success. The proportions are better than at Lincoln; the scale is much more imposing than at Wells. The arcade itself is indeed exactly right, and the clerestory is not without a certain coltish charm. The weak member is the tribune, which is much too squat: no eye could find much pleasure in such short, spreading openings. And the string-course at the base of the tribune, unfortunately not interrupted by any engaged shafts linking the piers to the vault, has become a hard unbroken line, as if drawn with a ruler and having, it seems, no connection with the arcade below it. Only in the transept end-elevations, where the tribune has given place to a triforium lighted by three pairs of windows, is this strong dark line a little easier to accept.

Ills. 68–70

Ill. 68

68 SALISBURY: The north transept

69 SALISBURY: The presbytery, looking south-east

70 SALISBURY: Interior, looking east

The decoration is plain. The tribune arches have some pierced tracery and some cusping, but stiff-leaf occurs only on the capitals of the retro-choir and on some of the bosses of the vault. Most of the Salisbury capitals, of the usual inverted-bell form characteristic of the Early English style, have only plain mouldings. On the other hand, the moulded arches, although not as rich as those at Wells, are fully comparable with Lincoln's; the alternating rolls and hollows yield, as usual, a light-and-shade effect which never fails to satisfy.

As a design it will be apparent that Salisbury, on balance, falls hardly if at all behind Lincoln and Wells. Why then is it so much less generally admired than they? Most people would reply: because it is so cold. What makes it so? In the first place there is the colour scheme. The creamy grey Chilmark oolite is rather light; the Purbeck shafting, of which there is a great deal, is, partly through having been artificially darkened with varnish, particularly black. This produces an over-emphatic contrast of tone as well as of colour. The perfection of the masonry helps to underline this impression. Such faultless precision seems, in this context, a little heartless. In Greece one would enjoy it, but in the North, and especially in the mediaeval North, one prefers a gentler handling. That nature, whether in human, animal or even foliate form, plays so small a part here only serves to enhance the feeling of aloofness. There is also the loss of nearly all the old glass. As far back as the early years of Elizabeth I great damage was done to the glass by a puritanical prelate, and Wyatt removed the rest. Because the architecture is so light and airy – the Purbeck stone piers in the Lady Chapel are the most slender in any English cathedral – the absence of old glass matters much more here than in some other cathedrals. The nave is so light that it holds no mystery, and to a mediaeval interior a certain degree of mystery may be a substantial asset. Nor must one other reason for the lack of warmth be forgotten: injudicious restoration.

It is proper to add that although Salisbury has no mystery and is deficient in texture, it has something else which on a sunny day can be very enjoyable: reflections. I do not know any other church in England in which, under the right conditions of light, the reflections count for so much. The crystalline clarity of the light in this building on a summer afternoon can also be seen to suit very well a design which was always distinguished above all for its lucidity.

The close, as a setting for a cathedral, is a purely English conception. On the continent of Europe it is not unusual to turn a corner and suddenly to be confronted with the immense mass of a cathedral soaring skywards. Little houses seem to be lapping its walls. If it is the church of the bishop, it is also the church of 'the folk'. In England, although at one time houses were built against York Minster, this is not the usual situation. Owing probably to the monastic origins of many of them, the English cathedrals tend to stand slightly apart from the rest of the town. Seldom are they at its centre; often, as at York or at Norwich, they are close to one corner of the original city, or, as at Durham and Lincoln, they are perched upon a hill overlooking the main part of the town. Again, as at Wells and Salisbury, they may be set back across the mown lawns of a large close, stately, gracious, self-contained and a little aloof. The exterior of Salisbury cathedral is seen to great advantage from its superb close, the finest in England. And here, a kind word can be said for Wyatt, for it was he who made the close as we now see it. He constructed drains to carry away the water from the steeply pitched cathedral roofs; he raised the whole expanse of the churchyard, levelled it, and removed the gravestones, a proceeding which in my view could be followed (with discrimination) more often.

Ills. 161, 171

Ills. 167, 8

Ills. 66, 67

In one respect the cathedral as originally conceived would have looked very different: the central tower would have been much less lofty, and its roof probably no more than a low pyramid, of wood. It will be evident that the present tower and spire, to which I shall return later, are disproportionately lofty. It will also be apparent that they are of such superb quality, and designed with such skill, that, miraculously, the cathedral is not overwhelmed but on the contrary greatly enhanced by this addition.

The west front is another example of the screen type of façade, and the least successful of any. Although clearly deriving from Wells, it is a sad travesty of its great prototype: a miscellany of small motifs which are nowhere co-ordinated. The large statues are all Victorian, and a very poor, insipid lot they are.

Ill. 67

Ill. 6 The east end is, as indicated earlier, a good instance of the stepped form. Beyond the east window of the sanctuary, there extend at a lower level a retro-choir and Lady Chapel. The stepped east end at Salisbury was conceived in this manner from the outset. The notion of clasping the gabled Lady Chapel between the gabled ends of the projecting choir aisles is charming, sensitive and original. The near view shows the profusion of set-offs which are another special characteristic of this design; excellent at ground-level (where they constitute a plinth) and below the windows, they seem less appropriate higher up on the buttresses. There is geometry everywhere: the gables, for example, are mostly equilateral triangles. The abundance of lancets, gables, finials and pinnacles creates a highly staccato, almost dancing rhythm, as remote as can be imagined from the slow solemn melodies of the cathedral architecture of a hundred years earlier.

The most characteristic feature of the English cathedrals during the middle part of the thirteenth century was without a doubt the lancet, which, sometimes pierced and glazed and sometimes blind, was employed in a wide range of different groupings. On the west front *Ill. 65* of Ripon the impact depends almost entirely upon lancets. It is rather a plain Jane, no doubt, and certainly too flat, but its very simplicity is appealing. It seems to have been finished about 1258. In 1379 the windows were all given traceries, which Scott about 1865 cut out, on the ground that they were badly decayed. For this he was much criticized, but this time I feel that aesthetically he was right. The location of the doors will seem surprising until it is realized that originally this church had no aisles, so that the towers projected beyond the side walls, just as they still do at Wells. Ripon, formerly in the diocese of York, did not attain cathedral status until 1836, and would not have achieved it then if geography had been less unkind to Beverley.

York itself, in the oldest portion that survives above ground, the great transepts, can show both fine and also rather indifferent examples of composition in lancets. The transepts were the major achievement of the long reign as archbishop (1215–1255) of Walter

71 YORK: The south transept and south-west tower

de Gray. Their size was important, for it gave the cue to later York builders to continue on an equally ambitious scale. Nearly 50 ft wide, their vault, had it ever been erected, would have soared to something like 110 ft. They were also aisled on both sides, which afforded scope, earlier than at Westminster Abbey, for transeptal façades in the French manner, but the opportunities were not taken.

The south transept front is exuberant: in some respects, indeed, *Ill. 71*

72 *left.* YORK: The 'Five Sisters' window in the north transept

73 *right.* YORK: Chapter-house, north transept and crossing-tower (an engraving of 1818 from Britton's *Cathedral Antiquities*)

over-exuberant; what *can* be the point of the three steep little gables over the doorway? But it differs from and, I am sorry to have to say, falls far behind contemporary France in several respects. The wheel-window is delightful, but it is placed too high. How much better if it had been below the base of the gable – the normal position in France – and larger. Weak, too, is the relationship between the centre-piece and the wings. The façade is conspicuously deficient in horizontal articulation. The lancets pop up all over the place. And where is the sculpture? In France such a front as this would have been profusely enriched. Here there is no carving at all, and it is sorely missed. So although lively, this south transept front cannot be accounted a success.

The north transept is in complete contrast. Both inside and out, this is perhaps the noblest lancet design in the country. All the fussy excitement of the south front has vanished; in this slightly later

work, completed about 1255, we have a design of the utmost serenity. Without and within, the composition is practically identical: a beautiful blind arcade below, unbroken by any doorway; five graduated lancets aloft, in the gable; and in between, the tallest mediaeval lancet-windows in England, each 5 ft wide and 53 ft high, the famous Five Sisters. These windows still contain some of their original glass; but so far from being a blaze of beautiful jewel-like colours, most of the glass is what is known as grisaille – greyish white glass upon which, with the aid of a neutral-coloured enamel used like paint and then fired into the glass, conventional stalk-and-leaf designs were carefully worked out. The effect is fine and, some might argue, more in tune than sparkling colour would be with the chaste, austere architecture; nevertheless I can never overcome my feeling that to sacrifice colour, in stained glass above all other media, implies an almost unbearable renunciation.

Ills. 72, 73

Lancets are also a leading architectural characteristic of Southwark, London's South Bank cathedral. (The diocese, created in 1905, covers the whole of South London and extends to the borders of Sussex.)
Ill. 74 Following a bad fire in 1207 the present choir may have been finished by about 1240. Although of modest proportions – only 55 ft from floor to vault – it is a well-knit design, clearly articulated both horizontally and vertically. There is no carved ornamentation at all, and there never was. The triforium arcade – and here it is a triforium, not a tribune – comprises continuous arches in each bay. The reredos is of much later date: it was set up about 1520, and the statuary is all Victorian. Originally there would have been a view
Ill. 123 beyond the high altar into the retro-choir, as there still is at Wells
Ill. 69 and now again, since the welcome removal of the reredos, at Salisbury. The Early English retro-choir, which serves also as an ambulatory surrounding the sanctuary, is the most generally admired feature of Southwark Cathedral.

The reader will perhaps have noticed that the parts of England which have so far played no part in our story are the West Midlands and North-West. For this the reasons were partly political and social: these were the least populous parts of the country in the Middle Ages and the poorest, and in most towns both the incentives and the resources for cathedral building were lacking. But another factor must also be taken into account: the material. Since transport in mediaeval times was so costly and, except by water, so arduous, builders naturally used a local stone wherever this was feasible, and the abbey and cathedral builders were no exception. Salisbury, Wells, Bristol, Gloucester, Oxford, Peterborough, Lincoln, York, Durham – all these are examples of churches which had the advantage of a good local stone (for the first seven, oolitic limestone; for York, magnesian limestone; for Durham, a tough carboniferous sandstone) close at hand. In the West Midlands and North-West, however, the local building stones were not so good. The four cathedrals in this part of the country, Worcester, Lichfield, Chester and Carlisle, were all built of friable New Red sandstone, and their masonry has suffered cruelly at the hands of time. All were, it is true, also war casualties

74 SOUTHWARK: The choir

in the seventeenth century; but the primary reason why these four cathedrals are less enjoyable to visit than for the qualities of their architecture they deserve to be is that, as Nikolaus Pevsner has said of Southwark, 'the restorers have relentlessly removed all those surface qualities which make a building lovable besides being respected.' Not that the thorough restorations of the Victorians were uncalled for: Pugin, in 1834, noted that the west front of Lichfield had been 'restored with brown cement, cracked in every direction'; a generation later Scott described the external stonework at Chester as 'so horribly and lamentably decayed as to reduce it to a mere wreck, like a mouldering sandstone cliff'. In many respects we owe a great debt to the Victorian restorers. Unhappily, however, they were prone not merely to replace but to 'improve'. Lord Grimthorpe's operations at St Albans were the most flagrant example, but the four New Red sandstone cathedrals also fared badly.

The redesigning and replacement a few years ago of most of the pretentious and trumpery Victorian fittings in the choir at Salisbury effected so great an improvement there that one hopes before long to see the same sort of work undertaken at Worcester, which is marred by a platitudinous screen, some very nasty seating, horrible floor-tiles and a lamentable (and all too prominent) reredos, as well as an abundance of indifferent stained glass. Yet the choir, eastern transepts and retro-choir here, begun in 1224, constitute the leading example of the mature Early English style of architecture in the West of England. Fifty years before, at the west end of the nave, two bays had been erected to a very curious design, a hybrid of Norman and Gothic, interesting but not artistically successful. The new design was very different: a work breathing self-assurance, in the triforium to the point of virtuosity. With such features as the profusion of lancets, the richness of mouldings, the wealth of stiff-leaf carving and lavish use of Purbeck marble we are already familiar, but in the triforium at Worcester there is a surprising innovation compared with which the arcade in two planes at Lincoln (see p. 92) is simple. Each bay contains, on the plane of the wall-face, a pair of arches, handsomely moulded and subdivided, with sculptures (unhappily all renewed) filling the tympanum above each subdivision. *Ill. 75*

75 WORCESTER: View into the north-east transept

All the shafts and abaci are of Purbeck marble. Behind runs a subsidiary arcade of lancet-shaped arches, smaller and lower so that it is fully seen; this establishes a complex and fascinating counterpoint which, except at the east end and transept ends, continues all round the eastern part of the cathedral at this level. The east end has been rebuilt, but the transept ends are original, and another triumphant example of composition in lancets. Again, at ground-level, there is a trefoiled arcade, whose spandrels once contained a very lively series of narrative sculptures: but vandals smashed most of them and they had to be extensively renewed.

This fine design is thought to have provided the inspiration for
Ill. 76 the chapter-house at Chester, one of the best features of a not very distinguished cathedral. Finished before 1250, this is a rectangular building which preserves its original vault. Its artistic appeal is mainly as a modest but rather elegant example of composition in lancets.

Meanwhile at Ely, under the enterprising Bishop Hugh Northwold (1229–1254), praised by Matthew Paris both for his piety and for his liberality, very beautiful additions were being made at the two ends of the cathedral. Mention has already been made of the Galilee
Ill. 25 porch (p. 49), built out in front of the west end. The side walls of the porch exhibit another variation on the interlocking arcade motif which we first met at Lincoln. Here the outer arches are effectively carried down to a lower plinth. The arcade, so airy, so graceful, so delicately conceived, is an exquisite enrichment of the wall-surface.

At the east end of the cathedral far more ambitious plans were afoot. As so often in the thirteenth century, the short apsed choir of the Romanesque building was proving much too small for the proper conduct of the services, so the bishop decided to add to the three Norman bays six more and a new east end. This extension, when it was finished in 1252, was the most sumptuous example of Gothic architecture in England. It is known both as the presbytery and, less correctly, as the retro-choir.

There can be no doubt that the primary source of inspiration for Bishop Northwold's presbytery was the nave of Lincoln, but it is even richer. The beautiful arcade is, once again, a little low, but the
Ill. 78 tribune is splendid: generous in scale and superbly ornamented. The

76 CHESTER: The chapter-house and crossing-tower, from the north-east

shafts, it need hardly be said, are again of Purbeck marble, introduced to add crispness and point to lines and other details. But since the piers between the paired arches are necessarily massive, the designer had the brilliant idea of separating the shafts by bands of sharply-cut trifoliate leaves. The paired arches are trefoiled, with cusps, and the three spandrels above have sunk quatrefoils on two planes, and sprays of foliage to either side of the central one. Yet despite all this elaboration the design, with its deeply recessed arches,

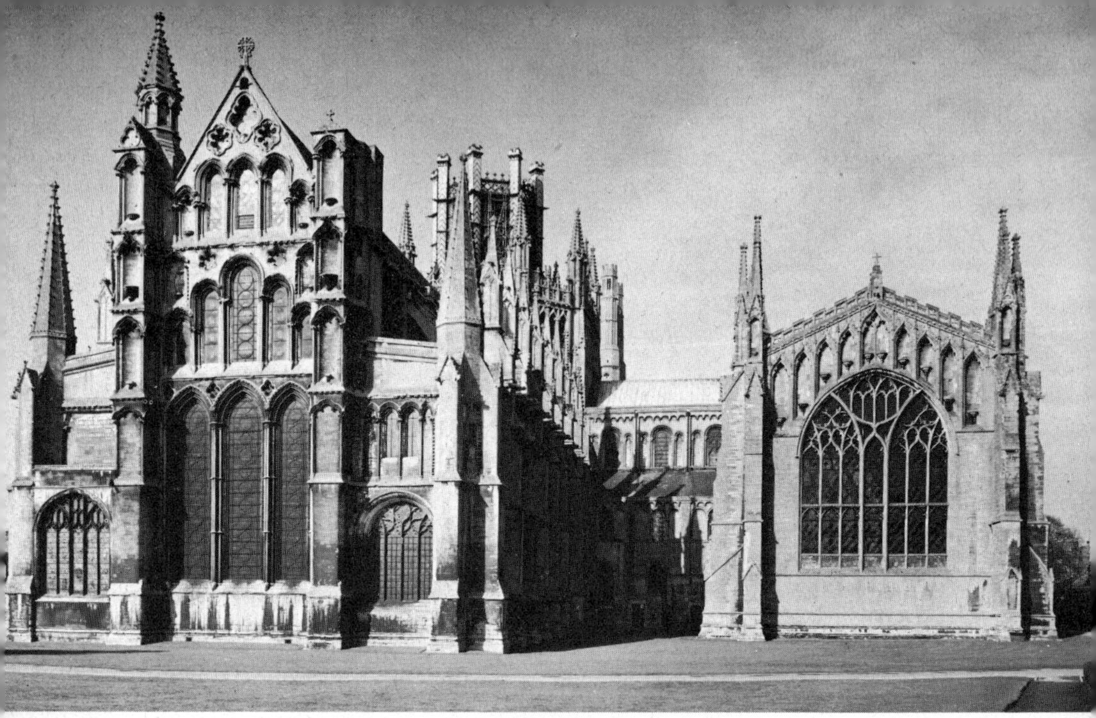

77 ELY: The east end and Lady Chapel

remains bold, giving an impression of immense self-assurance. Dog-tooth ornamentation occurs in the mouldings at all three levels, and especially in the clerestory. This, a triple-arched design, is delightful. It has more Purbeck shafting, arches of multi-foiled form and lancet windows set back deeply enough to leave room for a triforium-like passage. Finally there is the tierceron ribbed vault with strongly moulded ribs and large bosses, mostly stiff-leaf again, but including three with figure carvings. From the points of springing long triple clusters of engaged shafts sweep down to large ornamental corbels at the level of the arcade.

Ill. 77 The east end, in contrast to Salisbury, is an early example of the cliff-like kind, but the traceried window had not yet made its appearance, so instead we find an elaborate composition in lancets, of which the uppermost tier serves to light the vast roof that rises steeply over the vault. It is a pity that the aisle windows were subsequently altered.

78 ELY: The north side of the presbytery

So much importance was attached in this pious age to not interrupting the regularity of the services that, wherever possible, a new eastward extension would be complete, or nearly complete, before the Norman apses were taken down. Ely is an example of this; it *Ill. 79* also occurred at Durham, where in 1242 was begun a new east end unique in English cathedral architecture, the famous Chapel of the Nine Altars or eastern transept. The idea seems to have been taken from Fountains Abbey in Yorkshire, where the Cistercians had been building a similar large-scale transept in this position, the only other instance in England. The work at Durham proceeded slowly, and the chapel was not finished until about 1280.

The point of junction with the Norman building is decidedly awkward, but otherwise – although this east transept is so different in style from the rest of the cathedral – it harmonizes surprisingly well, perhaps because here too, as everywhere at Durham, the keynote is a robust vigour. (The feeble rose-window, inserted by Wyatt about 1795, has of course nothing to do with the original rose.) Particularly striking is the impression of strength conveyed by *Ill. 80* the tracery of the north window. Moving to one side and viewing

79 DURHAM: Air view, from the south-east

80 DURHAM: Chapel of the Nine Altars, looking north

the window obliquely, it becomes clear at once that this effect was most carefully contrived, by duplicating the principal tracery-bars. With this large window, which must have been the very last addition to the Chapel of the Nine Altars, we have moved out of the world of lancets, and are already in the full tide of Geometrical Decorated.

CHAPTER SIX

The Beginnings of Decorated

AT THE POINT of transition between the two phases of English Gothic architecture which, in Thomas Rickman's somewhat arbitrary terminology, now impossible to reject, are known as Early English and Decorated stands one of the finest of all England's churches: Westminster Abbey. Work began here in 1245 and went on continuously until 1269. Although not a cathedral, the abbey was in a position of special privilege, because it was the church of royal coronation and under royal patronage. Rheims, where the kings of France were crowned, had been consecrated in 1239. It was the moment when the fame of French church architecture had reached its apogee. English Gothic had been developing along very different lines, as has been evident at Wells, Lincoln, Salisbury and elsewhere; but King Henry III was an ardent Francophil, and architecturally Westminster Abbey represented a conscious return to French precedents. Any detailed consideration of the abbey would be outside the compass of the present book, but a few words must be said about the influence upon cathedral architecture of a church of such major importance.

At first sight this was much less than might have been expected. Specially French were the (for England) great height of the vault, 102 ft, and the *chevet*. Neither of these beautiful features was emulated elsewhere; English cathedral builders held on firmly to their flat east ends, and although they were to evolve ever more wonderful vaults, it is not for their loftiness that they are memorable. In two other less spectacular directions, however, the abbey pointed the way to innovations which were to be of far-reaching significance, and for both the source of inspiration was Rheims. There was the break-away from stiff-leaf to a more naturalistic kind of foliage carving: not a sudden change, but a gradual transformation characteristic of the third quarter of the thirteenth century. Still more

81 LICHFIELD: Interior, looking east

notable was the appearance at Westminster of bar window-tracery. Hitherto the only Gothic windows other than lancets had been of plate-tracery, which is easy to recognize, as the apertures, often lobed circles, always give the appearance of having been cut out of a solid wall of masonry. With bar-tracery, on the other hand, there is no suggestion of any solid stone in-filling within the window area; the window starts as a single large aperture, which is then filled with a skeleton of stone bars, at first always arranged in some sort of geometrical pattern. Hence the term frequently used to describe English Gothic in the latter part of the thirteenth century: Geometrical Decorated.

In addition to these general influences, the example of Westminster can be identified in a number of individual features in several cathedrals, as well as in one complete building, which will be described shortly. A very distinctive feature is the segmental window in the form of an equilateral triangle with curving sides, filled with three trefoil-cusped circles of bar-tracery. This unusual and attractive design was used for the tribune windows at Westminster and, very soon afterwards, for the clerestory of the nave at Lichfield. When it *Ill. 82*
was finished, about 1400, Lichfield must have been a cathedral of exceptional charm. Today, after incessant restoration, our enthusiasm must be more qualified. The choir, the transepts and the chapter-house were originally designed in the Early English style, but the choir in particular, fussily over-ornate, now appears to be mostly Victorian. The nave, which was building at the same time as Westminster Abbey, is much better. The height from floor to vault is a mere 57 ft, but the proportions are beautiful. As at Westminster, the *Ill. 81*
arcade absorbs half the total, but here the tribune and the clerestory divide the other half equally. Much of the nave vault is now only wood and plaster; farther east the vaulting has been extensively renewed, and, in the transepts at least, seems originally to have risen higher. Yet there is no denying the effectiveness of these vaults, which clearly derive from Lincoln.

The New Red sandstones are well known for their colour variations, even within the area of a single quarry. Lichfield Cathedral, externally, is orange-pink – more pink than orange; within,

82 LICHFIELD: View from the south aisle, looking north-east

most of the stone is fawn and very pale grey, with a blush of pale pink here and there. Thus it is not so much to its colour as to its linear richness that this building owes its interior warmth. That love of linear pattern which is so striking a characteristic of English Gothic was here carried a stage further. Particularly pleasing are the triple shafts which sweep up without interruption from floor to vault. On the way they bisect large cinquefoils within circles occupying the spandrels of the arcade: an invention as exquisite as it is unusual. An abundance of Early English dog-tooth enriches the arch mouldings of the tribune and the clerestory. On the other hand the capitals, both of the main arcade and at the springing-point of the vault, introduce, for good or ill, a naturalism such as has not *Ill. 83* previously been encountered: on the capital illustrated, the leaves and acorns are unmistakably oak. Another contributor to the warmth of Lichfield's interior is the trefoiled wall arcade which, as at Lincoln, runs gaily round below the aisle windows.

After the work on Westminster, suspended in 1269, the grandest example of English Gothic architecture in the second half of the thirteenth century was the new presbytery and retro-choir, always known as the Angel Choir, at Lincoln; to build this it was necessary to obtain from King Henry III a licence to demolish a portion of the city wall. The choir was begun – at the east end – in 1256, ostensibly to accommodate the crowds of pilgrims to the shrine of St Hugh.

83 LICHFIELD: A capital in the nave

84 **Lincoln:** The east end

Upon its completion in 1280, his relics were removed to a new position immediately behind the high altar. The east window, which measures about 59 ft by 29 ft, was astonishingly ambitious for its date, for it belongs to almost the earliest days of bar-tracery. It has often been admired, and its logic is irrefutable, but it is a somewhat tight, bookish design: a remarkable technical achievement but hardly, as some have claimed, a great work of art. In other respects this east front, despite its wealth of decorative enrichment, is not a success. The upper window, lighting the lofty roof area above the vault, is far too big; its head seems rammed up against the gable, and the way in which its base appears to be balanced on the tip of the window below is distinctly unhappy. The gables at the ends of the aisles, which incidentally are not of identical height, are also a dubious asset. Behind these gables the aisles have lean-to roofs.

Ill. 84

85 *left*. LINCOLN:
The Angel Choir, looking north-east

86 *right*. LINCOLN:
The Angel Choir, looking east

Seen from within, the big Geometrical window fills almost the whole of the central wall-space and certainly looks better than from without, although unfortunately the glass, dating from 1855, is unworthy. Nor are the points of junction between the east wall and those to north and south well managed. In other respects, however, the Angel Choir is one of the outstanding achievements of English Gothic. Reference to the preceding chapter will reveal at once how great was the debt to Bishop Northwold's presbytery at Ely, but this had itself owed much, as noted, to Lincoln's nave. The general proportions were predetermined, for it was decided at the outset that the Angel Choir should form a continuation eastwards of the ritual choir. The vault, therefore, is still too low; but it was possible to make two changes of marked aesthetic value: the arches of the main arcade rise slightly higher and are as much as 5 ft

Ill. 86

Ill. 85

narrower than those of the nave. The really novel feature, owing nothing to Ely, is the clerestory; with glorious extravagance, veils of open tracery rise in front of all the four-light windows, far enough away from them for a passage to run between. Such intricacy may seem confusing, but in fact it is sumptuous. It is from this clerestory that the designer of the north window of the Chapel of the Nine Altars at Durham (see p. 119) is thought to have taken his idea.

Ill. 87 In its ornamentation the Angel Choir is richer than the nave, richer even than the Ely presbytery; and although the applied colour and gilding characteristic of the time have long ago vanished, the effect is still enhanced by the sharp contrasts of tone and colour in the stone itself. The local brownish yellow limestone is an excellent foil for the dark Purbeck marble which was introduced here with a lavish hand – for as at Westminster some of the piers are wholly Purbeck. So are all the vigorously sprouting capitals of the main arcade. Otherwise the profuse decoration is nearly all in the lighter coloured limestone – the huge crocketed corbels supporting the vaulting shafts, the vertical bands of crockets (following Ely) between the Purbeck shafts which frame the three east windows and the north and south aisle windows and also adorn the piers of the tribune, the foliated hood-moulds of the tribune arches and their exceptionally bold capitals, the big dog-tooth ornamentation on the arches of the main arcade and the cusping of trefoils and quatrefoils at every level.

Ills. 88, 89 Besides all this there is the figure carving: a galaxy of heads, some exceptionally fine bosses, and the series of thirty angels in the spandrels of the tribune arcade which give this choir its name. For these the idea was taken from the transept ends at Westminster, where the four censing angels in the corner-spandrels are among the few English sculptures of the Middle Ages that can stand comparison with contemporary work in France. The Lincoln angels were clearly not all the work of the same sculptor: some are angelic musicians, whereas others, cast in a sterner mould, have a doctrinal significance. It would be good to be able to say that either group was the artistic equal of Westminster or of typical French sculpture of the period, but to do so would be to strain the truth.

87 LINCOLN: The Angel Choir. Detail of tribune and clerestory

88, 89 LINCOLN: The Angel Choir. Details of sculpture

Ill. 90 While the Angel Choir was building, a somewhat unusual feature was added farther west, in the form of a pair of stone doorways from the great transepts into the choir aisles. Both for their design and for their ornamentation, these rank among the supreme beauties of Lincoln. For their contrasts of light and dark, of plain and intricate surfaces, of abstract and naturalistic decoration, it would scarcely be possible to imagine designs of more inevitable rightness or surpassing distinction. The broad mouldings here, marvellously undercut, are less naturalistic and probably a little earlier than the Lichfield capital, but already the familiar stiff-leaf is in process at last of giving way before the closely packed leaves of an English hedgerow. The ends of these broad mouldings harbour, on the north doorway, strange

90 *right*. LINCOLN: Doorway to north choir aisle

91 *below*. LINCOLN: Detail from the doorway to south choir aisle

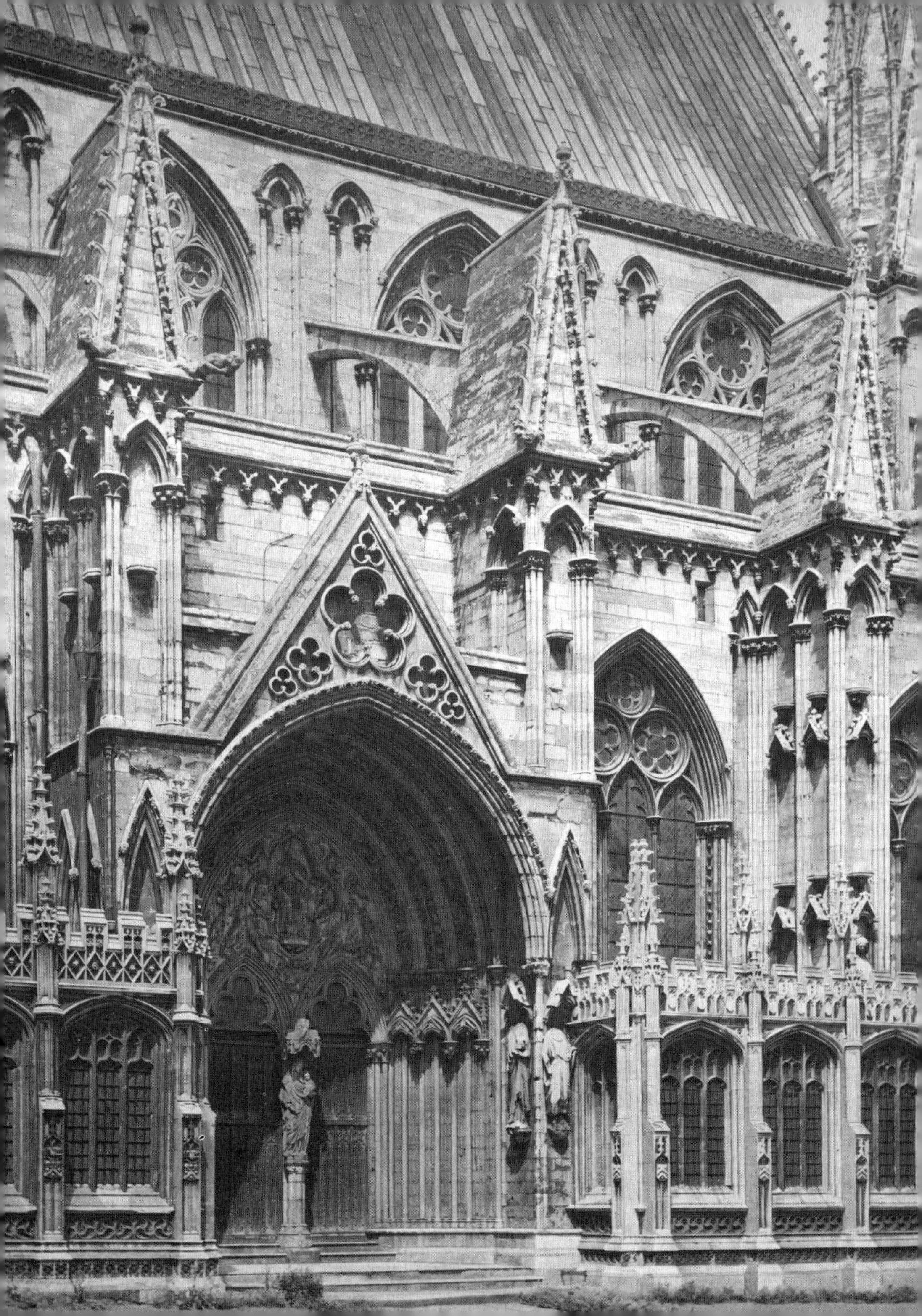

dragons, half-hidden among the foliage; on the other door the dragons inhabit the capitals, as do little figures of standing men and, on the side not shown, owls. All this is carving of delicious quality. Ill. 91

The Angel Choir also has important external sculptures, mainly on the south side. The small scale of most English Gothic doorways – those at Wells being but an extreme instance – was usually such as to preclude the kind of sculptural accompaniment which became practically *de rigueur* in France. But the south-east porch at Lincoln, usually known as the Judgment porch, was an exception. Today this porch is flanked by a pair of Late Gothic chantry chapels which were of course no part of the original design. The four large figures on the buttress piers have lost their heads; the Virgin and Child on the central pier (the *trumeau*) is new; the tympanum has been much restored, especially the seated figure of Christ as Judge and the pair of angels within the recessed quatrefoil, all now somewhat insipid. The over-all design, however, is unaltered and is of interest as owing little or nothing to France. Instead of a series of horizontal zones there is a general sense of flutter, closer in spirit to book illumination, from which it may perhaps have been derived. The jaws of Hell, wide open to receive the luckless damned, are in the central spandrel, immediately below the quatrefoil. Ill. 92

Surrounding the tympanum are three unrestored orders of voussoirs, separated by mouldings of great delicacy. The inner arch contains a series of canopied figures of kings and queens, six of each, probably introduced as ancestors of Christ. The second arch has undercut foliage of filigree quality, unfortunately a good deal damaged, while the outer order has figures again: on the right eight male figures believed to be apostles, and on the left some of the wise and foolish virgins. These figures, although small in scale, are among the finest at Lincoln, and so close in spirit and in accomplishment to the best of the Westminster sculptures that it has been supposed that one or more of the royal carvers may have been brought up from London to undertake the work. Specially happy is the way in which the figures, instead of projecting, are set back within bowers of exquisitely undercut foliage, which greatly enrich without in any way impinging upon the lines of the architecture. Ill. 93

92 LINCOLN: South-east or 'Judgment' porch

93 *left.* LINCOLN:
Detail from the south-east porch

94 *right.* LINCOLN:
Queen Margaret of Valois (?)

Close also to Westminster in style is the life-size figure usually *Ill. 94* known as Queen Margaret of Valois, the second wife of Edward I. She stands under one of the canopies on the first buttress to the east of the Judgment porch, and would seem to owe her preservation from the fanaticism of later iconoclasts to the fortunate accident of having been pinned in by the parapet of the later chantry chapel. Margaret became queen in 1299; if the association of this statue with her were correct, it would therefore mean on the one hand that this was one of the latest sculptures at Lincoln and on the other that it was one of the earliest of England's portrait statues, but unfortunately there is nothing to prove the identification. At one time even the authenticity of the head was questioned, but it is in fact a work of great accomplishment, combining in a high degree dignity and grace. It is a pity that it is so obscurely placed that many people overlook its existence or, if they do find it, are unable to see it as it deserves to be seen.

The cloisters at Lincoln were not begun until 1296. They were a late addition here because in cathedrals served by secular canons they were unnecessary. In northern France one scarcely ever finds them, and not always in England: York, for example, has never possessed any cloisters, nor has Lichfield. For the monastic cathedrals they were indispensable, and they were felt to be such an agreeable accessory that several of the non-monastic cathedrals added them, for the sheer pleasure they provide: and what better reason can be imagined? In so far as they served a function in the non-monastic cathedrals, it was for processional purposes; this explains why at some of these, such as Wells and Chichester, the cloister walk adjacent to the nave was omitted. This economy was not practised at Salisbury, where in the 1270s cloisters were added on a princely scale: these are the largest and, with the exception of Gloucester, the finest cloisters in England, as well as being the earliest to survive in their present form. Four spacious walks, all with simple quadripartite vaults, open upon a garth in which today grow two magnificent cedars. The traceried arcades are a splendid example of Early Geometrical Decorated, greatly enhanced by the dark shadows against which they are habitually seen. The decay of the original Purbeck marble shafts and their replacement by lighter ones was

Ills. 95, 96

95 SALISBURY: The cloisters

96 SALISBURY: The south side of the nave, with the cloisters

certainly all to the good. Each bay has two pairs of gracefully designed sub-openings, with large circles filled with cinquefoils and sexfoils in alternation, resting on their arches. Such amplitude of design makes the lancets of the church look positively ascetic.

The usual position for the chapter-house was on the east side of the cloisters, which means that it is often, as here, immediately south of the south transept. The Salisbury chapter-house was not merely inspired by Westminster but closely copied from that illustrious building. From 1282 to 1547 the meeting-place of the Commons of England, the Westminster chapter-house has been greatly restored: the doorway, the central pier, the whole of the vault and the conical roof (constructed of iron, but welcome) are all due to George Gilbert Scott. At Salisbury there is no tent roof, and it is a pity.

97 SALISBURY: The chapter-house (an engraving of 1814 from Britton's *Cathedral Antiquities*)

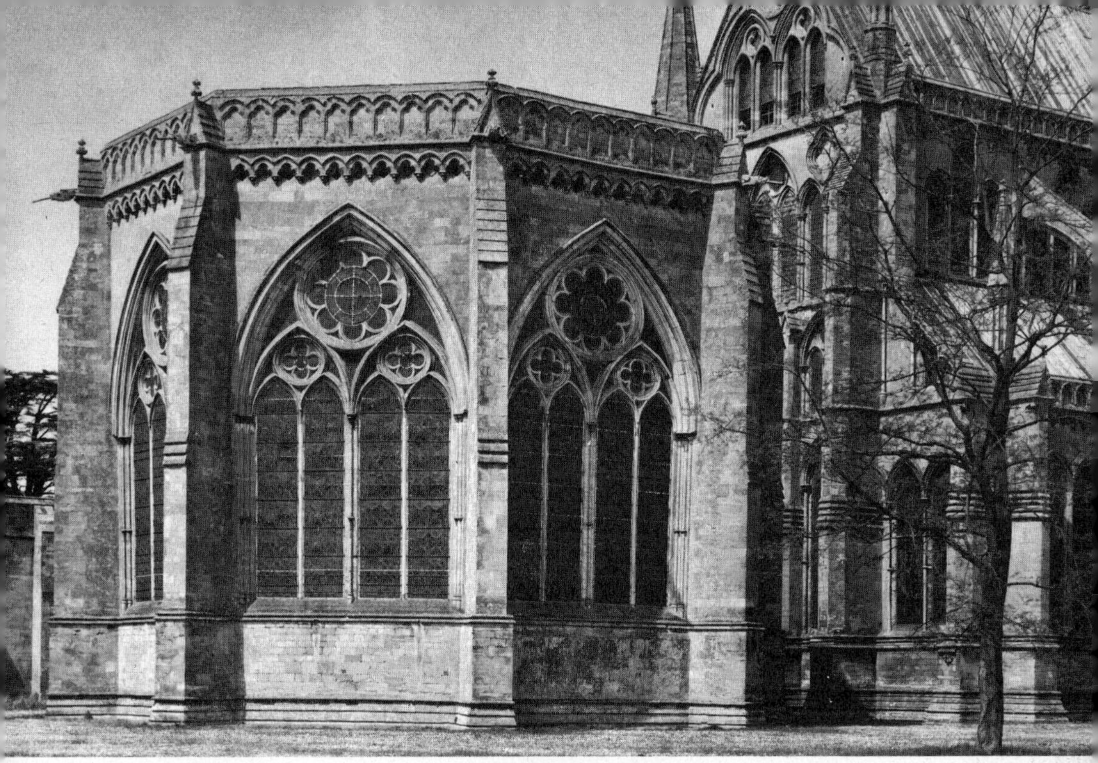

98 SALISBURY: The chapter-house. Exterior, from the south-east

Internally the impression is all too Victorian. The windows of 1862 have in recent years been a subject of controversy: their leading and grisaille patterns are passable, but the glass itself gives no pleasure. Worse still are a detestable glazed floor and inept painted decoration on the vaulting, much inferior to some original work still remaining in the antechamber. The Old Testament narrative sculpture in the spandrels of the wall arcade is over-restored but interesting. Structurally, despite everything, this interior is still very fine; the central pier, surrounded by eight free-standing colonnettes of Purbeck marble, shoots up like a stalk before dividing into sixteen branches, which help to support an ingenious and beautiful vault. Externally, undistracted by the glass, one can enjoy to the full the splendid windows, with their huge octofoiled circles rising above pairs of smaller circles with quatrefoils, directly inspired, again, by the similar but sexfoiled windows of Westminster.

Ill. 97

Ill. 98

The Manor of Southwell, in Nottinghamshire, was for nearly nine hundred years a possession of the Archbishops of York; it was they who founded the college of secular canons there, and it was they who were responsible for all the buildings. Only since 1884 has Southwell formed a separate see. Its most celebrated building is the chapter-house, erected during the last decade of the thirteenth century. There are no cloisters, and the approach is from an arcaded vestibule. The building itself is again octagonal, and has kept its high conical roof *Ill. 23* sheathed with lead, but it is so much smaller than Salisbury or Westminster (with a diameter of 31 ft instead of about 58 ft) that the builders were able to dispense with the central pier. The windows are also smaller, but their tracery design is subtle and complex. The material is a fine-grained magnesian limestone quarried near Mansfield, about fifteen miles away.

It was no doubt this stone which helped to render possible the carving of the famous leaves of Southwell, one of England's cathedral glories. They decorate the capitals and gables of the chapter-house and vestibule wall arcades and two of the arch mouldings of *Ill. 99* the exquisite doorway. A glance at the general disposition of the foliage carving will provide the key to all the decoration at Southwell. It is at once exuberant and disciplined – strictly confined, that is to say, within certain areas. Most of the leaves here are quite easy to identify, yet although nature has been followed so closely the decorative aspect is never for a moment overlooked. In this doorway the unornamented parts obviously play a vital role in the design as a whole.

Within the chapter-house are thirty-six stalls, each with a gable *Ill. 100* rising above a sharply pointed trefoil arch. Here too there are leaves, both in the form of crockets and of decorative designs within the spandrels, all executed with wonderful crispness. Some of the corbels from which the gables spring are in the form of human heads, whose carving is so vivid as to suggest portraiture; one wonders, in fact, whether that on the left of the photograph is not a self-portrait of the master-carver himself. The capitals, on the other hand, are foliated throughout, giving the impression that the sculptors – and there were at least three of them – stepped out into

99 SOUTHWELL: The entrance to the chapter-house

100 *above*. SOUTHWELL: The chapter-house. Stall canopies

101–104 *right*. SOUTHWELL: Capitals from the chapter-house and its vestibule

the surrounding fields and woods and came back with freshly gathered bunches to serve as their models. Among the leaves represented are the oak, the maple, the hop, the vine and the ivy, white bryony, hawthorn, whitethorn, wild apple, wild rose, potentilla and buttercup. In nature, of course, these leaves vary considerably in size, but at Southwell scale was very properly disregarded in the interest of artistic unity, so that the small leaf of the hawthorn appears to be the same size as the large leaf of the vine. It is no surprise to discover that one of the finest of the capitals crowns the central shaft of the double-arched entrance, a place of special prominence doubtless reserved for the master-carver. His choice was the buttercup, which sprouts up with a bursting sense of life. There are a few flowers, but the leaves provide the principal theme, and they are disposed here with variety but also with admirable lucidity in two tiers. The depth of the undercutting and the resultant shadows are an invaluable foil for the rich surface texture.

Ills. 101–104

101 Hop

102 Hawthorn

103 Vine and Ivy

104 Buttercup

Ill. 102 Above the hawthorn capital is more hawthorn, surrounding a somewhat mask-like face. This is the Jack-in-the-Green, or Green Man, who occurs not infrequently in mediaeval art, and whose memory survives in the numerous 'Green Man' public houses to be found all over England. The face was that of a youth, or occasionally of a maiden, who was otherwise entirely covered with foliage to portray the spirit of a tree. Thus personified, the tree-spirit was led through the fields with traditional ceremony to encourage fertility. It was certainly a custom of pagan origin, but the tradition died hard, and it is interesting to find that the ecclesiastical authorities did not try to suppress it but allowed it to become a familiar motif of church decoration.

Looking at the Southwell sculpture as a whole, some people may be tempted to wonder whether so close an adherence to natural forms did not imply, inevitably, an artistic decline. Where now, they may ask, are those qualities of imagination and inward, personal fantasy which make Romanesque sculpture at its best (one is bound to add, at its comparatively rare best) so precious? I am in no doubt about the answer: there was a decline. The leaves of Southwell are not on the same artistic level as, say, the finest of the capitals in the Canterbury crypt. But the fairer confrontation, in my view, would be with Grinling Gibbons, whose work at St Paul's,

105 SOUTHWELL:
The chapter-house.
Star-vault

106 SOUTHWELL:
The chapter-house.
Central roof boss

London, we shall meet in a later chapter; and in this comparison the mediaeval work fully holds its own. Both the Grinling Gibbons group of carvers and the Southwell group show a high regard for the decorative aspect; the work of both is so much a part of the architecture to which it belongs that we are untroubled, and indeed delighted, by the naturalism. *Ill. 188*

In the vault of the Southwell chapter-house, completed only very shortly after the capitals and stall-gables – that is to say just about 1300 – a change can already be detected. The absence of any central pier left the way open for the construction of an exquisite star-vault. There can be no doubt that the bosses of this vault were the work of another, and probably younger, carver. The central boss is very large. It is also joyous; yet already one can detect the beginning of a movement away again from nature in the direction of something more standardized – the typical bubbly foliage of the fourteenth century, as Lawrence Stone has termed it. Of course it had not gone very far yet, but all the leaves on the boss are much alike and difficult to identify with certainty, so that one's first thoughts now are of pattern, of all-over pattern, rather than of species, of individual species. Here the result is still delightful; but at the end of this road lay the so-called four-leaved flower of Perpendicular ornament, which could be rebarbatively mechanical. *Ill. 105* *Ill. 106*

CHAPTER SEVEN

The Flowering of Decorated

WE HAVE NOW reached the first half of the fourteenth century, which is undoubtedly one of the most brilliant periods in the history of English architecture. In contrast to France, this was in England an age of growing economic prosperity. By 1300 the Church was already the repository of unrivalled wealth, which provided a continual incentive to rebuild and to beautify. There was, moreover, as Joan Evans has explained,[8] a special reason why so much of this treasure now went into buildings. In 1297 Edward I, contemplating the possibility of a war with France, appointed commissioners whose task it was to make inventories of all ecclesiastical and monastic treasures, in case the King should need them to pay for his military adventures. This was something of a shock to the churchmen, and left them with a feeling that portable objects were not a very safe investment. A fine building, lavish sculpture, elaborate woodwork, abundant stained glass – these were better because they lent themselves less easily to expropriation. So up went the churches, one after another, and many already there, including cathedrals, were magnificently enriched.

The Decorated cathedral *par excellence* is Exeter. The rebuilding of this church, begun between 1275 and 1280, spans the whole of the first half of the fourteenth century and some twenty years before and after. It was not, for once, the aftermath of any disaster. Many Romanesque towers had collapsed, but never these; and there had been no fire. The rebuilding of Exeter was the work of a succession of enterprising bishops who simply wanted their cathedral to be more up-to-date and more beautiful; one of them at least provided a large part of the funds out of his own pocket. Apart from the towers the rebuilding was comprehensive and in accordance with a uniform design, so that Exeter displays greater stylistic consistency than any other pre-Reformation English cathedral except Salisbury.

107 WELLS: The retro-choir, looking north-east

Nevertheless, its present form was to a considerable extent determined by its Norman predecessor. The decision to retain the not very lofty towers is probably the main reason for the lowness of this building. Had it risen to the height of, say, Salisbury, it would have dwarfed them. A good deal of Norman walling was also retained, and this explains why the dimensions both of the nave and choir were left unchanged. Only the presbytery and Lady Chapel at *Ill. 108* the east end were entirely new. These are well seen in the view from the air.

The exterior of Exeter Cathedral is, however, of small account by comparison with the interior. And since it was served by a chapter of secular canons, the ancillary buildings were also less important than in the monastic cathedrals. Cloisters were added later, but they have not survived. The most striking characteristic of the plan, also evident from the air photograph, is its symmetry. The two towers, each with its east-facing chapel, match exactly; farther east are four more projecting chapels, again in pairs.

To step into Exeter Cathedral is to enjoy another of the supreme *Ill. 109* architectural pleasures of England. Although the nave was not built until the 1330s and was not vaulted until about thirty years later, the design, except of the sculptural detail, follows so closely that of the choir and presbytery, which were erected between 1288 and 1309, that in spirit all belong to the opening years of the fourteenth century. The pulpitum, aesthetically very necessary here, is a charming work of about 1320; originally there was only a central opening, but the unusual idea of piercing through the solid wall on the choir side to make two more apertures was a very happy one. The organ-case is better than some, but in my view the organ is excessively obtrusive. More to be regretted internally is that the vault rises to a mere 69 ft. Height, although exciting, is not an end in itself; what matters is proportion. At Exeter the vault, once again, is too low for its width and especially for its length, for this is the longest church roof in England – just 300 ft – flowing through from end to end without a break, since there is no central tower to interrupt it.

There is little else to criticize. The special delight of this interior resides in its exceptional warmth. This sensation stems, of course, from the multiplication of shafts (sixteen to each pier), mouldings (eightfold on the main arches) and vault ribs. The stone itself adds still further to the impression of richness, for it is of several different kinds and colours. The Dean and Chapter owned a limestone quarry at Beer, some twenty miles along the coast from Exmouth. The whitish parts of the walls are of this stone, as are the vault ribs except at their lower ends; but Beer stone is cretaceous and comparatively soft, and it was not regarded as trustworthy enough for the piers. So these were built of Purbeck, a stone with which we are by this time very familiar. Here, however, it was left unpolished and looks much lighter: a medium grey, in fact. In addition to these there is a yellowish sandstone which was used for the arches of the arcade, the corbels and the bosses, while the local red sandstone was employed for the core of the walls, behind the facings, in the form of rubble embedded in thick mortar.

108 EXETER: Air view, from the south-east

109 Exeter: Interior, looking east

Looking more closely at the elevation, it will be seen not only that the tribune has gone (and for good) but that the middle stage, even as a triforium, has not the importance which it had in the thirteenth century, either in scale or in function, for there is no through passageway at this level. The upper part, with a double tier of pierced quatrefoils, is a parapet which really belongs to the clerestory, for it is here that the passage runs. This is a pointer to the future. For the closer identity of these two upper stages, carried sometimes, as we shall see, to the point of complete amalgamation or of total suppression of the triforium, is a frequent characteristic of later Gothic designs. It was a pity. The three-stage ordonnance is unquestionably more beautiful than the two; the blind stage provides an aesthetically important interval of repose between the coloured windows above and below. We can be glad therefore that at Exeter the triforium, although reduced to four dainty trefoil-headed arches in each bay, was not entirely suppressed. The clerestory, by contrast, is now large, and nearly the whole of the area in each bay is filled by a single large window. The window traceries attain a complexity beyond anything that we have encountered so far, and the debt to France is beyond question. Yet the majority of the tracery patterns still remained Geometrical rather than Flowing. The essential difference is that, in the former, the geometrical figures – circles, trefoils, quatrefoils and so on – appear to be resting either on or between the pointed heads of the window lights, whereas in the Flowing type the mullions are themselves carried into the pattern of the tracery, swinging to and fro in reverse curves and ogees. There is no example of fully developed Flowing tracery at Exeter, but here and there the beginnings of the new style are apparent; in the large
Ill. 112 west window it can be seen that the Catherine wheel has started to turn.

One of the nave clerestory windows is blocked, for the fifth bay from the west on the north side contains the well-known Minstrels'
Ill. 110 Gallery. This would appear to belong to about the middle of the fourteenth century. The ornamentation has been laid on so thickly that, like Devonshire cream, it has become clotted. Under those lofty canopies which are also characteristic of the stained glass

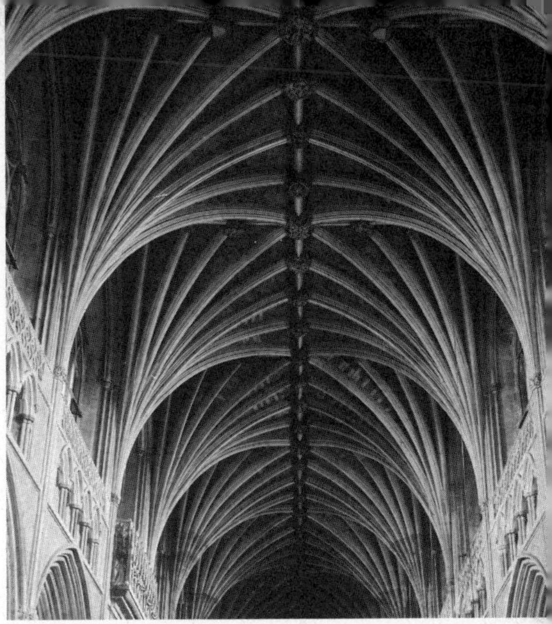

110 EXETER: The Minstrels' Gallery

111 EXETER: The nave vault

of this date stand fourteen angels (including the two on the ends facing east and west), each playing a musical instrument. Sculpturally it cannot be said that these rather doll-like figures rank high, but they are pretty and gay; like much carved stonework at Exeter, they have been recoloured and regilded.

The glory of Exeter is beyond doubt the vault. The effect has often been compared to an avenue of stately trees. Along the central axis, the arrangement of the ribs – transverse, tierceron, diagonal, tierceron, transverse in each bay – is as at Lincoln, although the ribs here are thicker and project more boldly. The new feature is the elaboration towards the windows. In each bay supplementary ridge-ribs now run crosswise, from window-head to window-head, with as many as six pairs of tiercerons rising to each. The tremendous sculptured bosses, so much larger than they need have been if their sole function had been to hide the joins, add a further note of luxuriance. Every rib, moreover, rises from the point of springing, and thus all appear to serve a structural and not merely a decorative purpose. Francis Bond described Exeter as having 'the finest and most complete quadripartite vault in existence'. *Ill. 111*

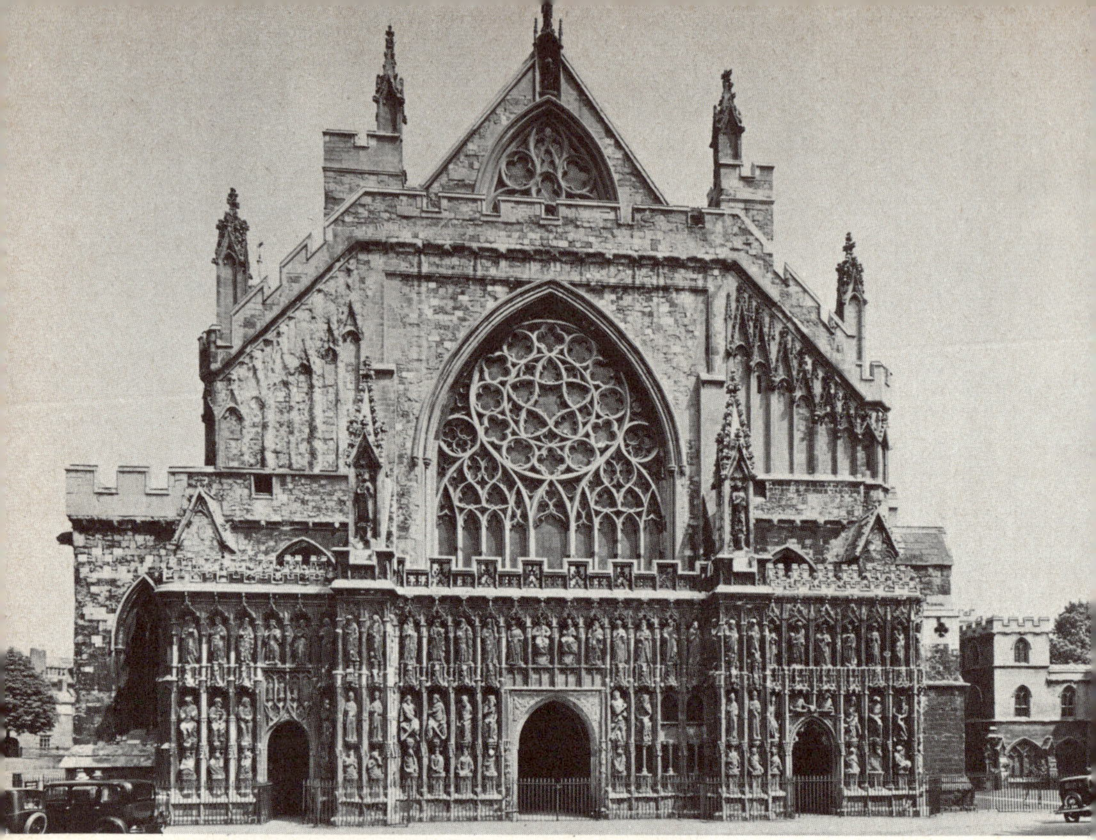

112 *above*. EXETER: The west front

113 *left*. EXETER: Statues from the west front

114 *right*. LINCOLN: Statues from the west front

The west front is a curious composition dating from about 1346–1375. It is designed in three planes, which seem to impinge on one another, and although by no means without interest, can hardly be termed an artistic success. The lower part, with the sculpture, has the effect of a screen which is not integral; although it followed on immediately after the completion of the rest, it seems that it was indeed an afterthought. The masking of the base of the west window, which was already too short for its width, is very unfortunate, while the window in the gable, lighting the roof-area above the vault, peers oddly over the upper line of battlements like a face. The tracery of both windows, however, is well worth studying. The sculptures have the merit of being largely unrestored work of about 1375, but most of them are sadly weather-worn. Informality is now the key-note. Various notabilities (the two illustrated are said to be Count Stephen and Godfrey of Bouillon) sit cross-legged, in amiable conversation. They are certainly lively, but considered formally, they are very ungainly, and all dignity has vanished. A somewhat similar gallery of seated kings was added a few years later to the centre of the west front at Lincoln. These are no less informal in their poses, but better proportioned, and, because of the superior quality of the stone, much better preserved.

Ill. 112

Ill. 113

Ill. 114

The long duration of the rebuilding operations at Exeter has taken us well beyond the period with which this chapter is principally concerned, and it is now time, retracing our steps, to turn to the second of the three most important cathedral enterprises belonging to the half century or so before the Black Death: Wells east of the
Ill. 115 central crossing and including the chapter-house. This latter building is unusual in being above ground-level, and is therefore approached
Ill. 116 by a stone stairway. In the photograph the entrance to the chapter-house is on the right. Straight ahead is the bridge over the Chain Gate to the Vicars' Close, not built until the mid-fifteenth century. Thus the double-branching, to which the stair owes its fame, was in a sense a lucky accident. Two of the vaulting shafts spring from
Ill. 117 charming corbels. One has a monk holding on (understandably) with one hand while with the other he thrusts a stick down the throat of a dragon. It is admittedly a very mild dragon; but in the Decorated period everybody, even a dragon, was amiable.

The chapter-house, octagonal in shape and a little smaller than Salisbury or Westminster but much better preserved, is architec-

115 WELLS: Air view, from the east

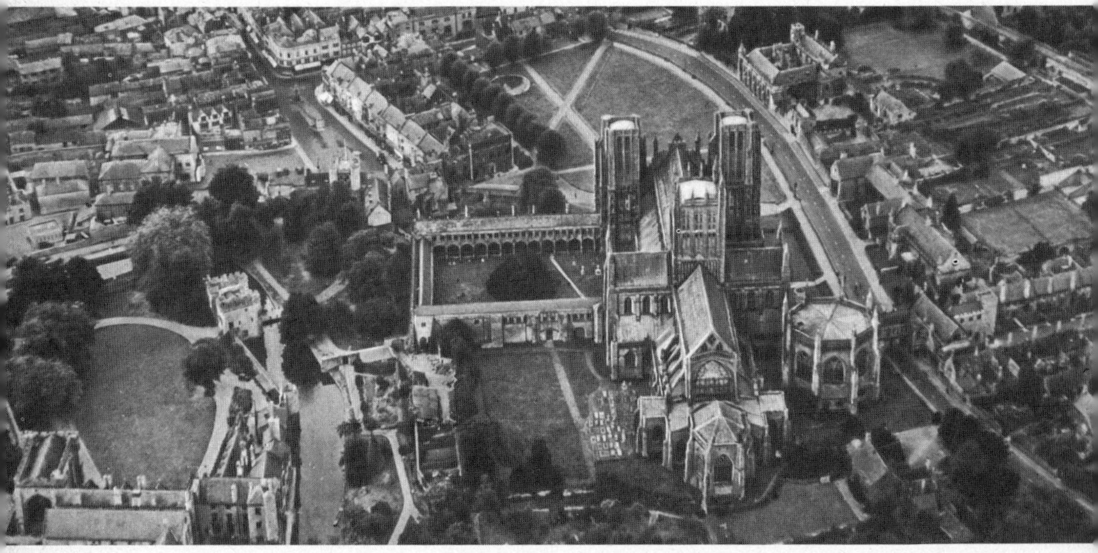

turally the most beautiful in England. It was finished not later than 1319. Below the windows runs an arcade with fifty-one stalls, whose canopies are alive with heads of kings, churchmen and others, many smiling or even laughing. Such light-hearted gaiety would have been inconceivable in the Romanesque period. This happy spirit is communicated by the structure too, and by the glass; for though the bulk of the original glazing of Edward II's time has gone, there is still quite a lot in the tracery lights, which sparkle with ruby and white. The tracery here is still Geometrical, but the windows, which are large, are abundantly adorned with the ball-flower, a formalized floral ornament as characteristic of the first half of the fourteenth century as the dog-tooth was of the thirteenth. Truly thrilling is the vault, which surpasses even Exeter, from which it obviously derives, in its exuberance. From the central stalk there radiate no less than thirty-two ribs, mostly tiercerons, and at each point of meeting there is a carved foliage boss. The effect is marvellously rich. The analogy with a great palm tree is difficult to resist, and seldom has been.

Ill. 119

116 WELLS: Stairway leading to the chapter-house

117 *above*. WELLS: Corbel on the wall of the chapter-house stairway

Nevertheless, in the profile of the central pier a subtle change can be detected which is not altogether for the better. The essential departure from Early English practice is that, whereas the colonnettes are more numerous than ever, they now have less projection. There is therefore less play of light and shade over the surface, but instead a continuous ripple. A perpetual undulation in the handling of all the linear elements, already evident in pier profiles and arch mouldings and soon to be seen in window-tracery too, is specially characteristic of the flowering of Decorated. Nor does the rippling foliage project so boldly as in thirteenth-century work. The English cathedrals of the later Decorated period have, on capitals, corbels and bosses, plenty of foliage carving, but with rare exceptions it is neither so vital nor so effective as the best stiff-leaf or as the triumphant nature-worship at Southwell.

Ill. 118

Before the chapter-house at Wells was complete, work had started on the Lady Chapel. The air view shows the elevated chapter-house on the right and the Lady Chapel, stepping down towards the east as usual in this part of England. This building is an elongated

Ill. 115

119 *right.* WELLS: The chapter-house vault

118 *below.* WELLS: A capital in the retro-choir

120 WELLS: The Lady Chapel vault

octagon, which has the effect of mitigating to some extent the bluntness of the usual English east end. It was at first intended to be a separate building, but this scheme was soon altered, and a retro-choir was introduced between the presbytery and the Lady Chapel.

Ill. 121 The cross-view, apart from other beauties, is valuable for the light it throws on the development of window-tracery in the few years between, say, 1315 and 1325. The window on the right is a good example of the Flowing type. The much larger east window of the Lady Chapel, seen on the left, is no longer purely Geometrical, but too hesitant as yet to be described as Flowing. Both windows are examples of the kind of Decorated tracery known as Reticulated. In this type one pattern is repeated over the whole area, which can be very satisfying when the window is not so large that the tracery design becomes monotonous.

The Lady Chapel has five large windows, all but one of which are filled with fragments of early fourteenth-century glass – mainly golden brown, olive-green, ruby, blue and white: a kaleidoscope of

Ill. 120 glorious colours. The fascinating star-vault may be compared with

Ill. 105 that of the Southwell chapter-house, for here at Wells is one of the earliest examples in England of a lierne-vault. It is the short ribs that

121 WELLS: View from the retro-choir south aisle, looking north-east into the Lady Chapel

do not spring from the capital, nor, necessarily, rise to the central ridge, which give their name to this type of vault. Such liernes, as they are called, fulfil no structural purpose, but by crossing and recrossing the more functional ribs they were able to produce decorative patterns, sometimes of great beauty. There will be much more to say about lierne-vaults in the pages that follow.

Ill. 122 If now, standing in the Lady Chapel, we turn westwards, we find ourselves face to face with one of the most subtle and entrancing architectural prospects in England. The notion of linking the Lady Chapel to the presbytery by inserting between them a retro-choir while preserving the chapel's polygonal form was hazardous, but it turned out to be a stroke of genius. The vistas are pure poetry. Slender reed-like shafts of dark marble are applied here for almost the last time in a mediaeval building to add tonal accents to the piers (two of which are triangular on plan) at carefully judged intervals. The arrangement of the arches and of the many-ribbed vaults is
Ill. 107 markedly complex, and allows of some fascinating cross-vistas.

122 WELLS: The retro-choir seen from the Lady Chapel

123 WELLS: The presbytery, looking east

The idea of the retro-choir was to have somewhere to house the relics of a saint, which by the end of the thirteenth century, as Canterbury and Lincoln bear witness, had become a very profitable asset. But the problem at Wells was to produce the saint. They had no one. In the end the selected candidate, Bishop de la Marchia (d. 1302), failed to qualify for canonization. So the retro-choir remained untenanted.

The 1330s saw the reconstruction of the late-twelfth-century choir and its extension to embrace a new presbytery. Unhappily the choir was largely done over again about 1850 by Salvin and today, thanks to its Victorian appointments, is aesthetically much the weakest part of the cathedral. But it is only three bays long. The presbytery, also
Ill. 123 of three bays, is far finer, and the view eastwards, through the retro-choir into the Lady Chapel, is an outstanding example of Decorated complexity. There is no triforium here. Instead, the wall-surface above the arcades was given a generous mantle of tabernacle work: statues (renewed) stand on pedestals under canopies, separated by slender shafts projecting in pairs. In a building as low as Wells, this strongly vertical emphasis is of special value. The wall passage is at the clerestory level. The whole scheme presages that liking for panelled surfaces so characteristic of Perpendicular Gothic. In the tracery of the east window, not on analysis a very pleasing design, there is also a hint of Perpendicular, but in its glass this, the famous Golden Window, with a Tree of Jesse as its subject, is pure Decorated, and the finest of its period in England. The vault, which covers both choir and presbytery, is again of the lierne kind, but quite different from that of the Lady Chapel. There are no diagonal ribs now and none at the ridge; instead the pattern of ribs suggests a net, suspended over the entire space with little regard for the separate bays. Curious too are the cusps in the squares and in some of the lozenges: they look like large thorns.

These same wonderful years at Wells saw the rebuilding of the central tower, of which more will be said in the following chapter, as the design was a good deal modified about 1440. Here unfortunately the builders overreached themselves; their tower was too heavy for its foundations and abutments, and alarming settlements occurred almost at once. To prevent a total collapse, massive
Ill. 124 scissor-arches were constructed in 1338 under the north, south and west tower arches. Structurally this bold expedient was a great success; the tower still stands, most of it now nearly 650 years old, and has never since given cause for anxiety. But what is to be said of the appearance of these arches? Although their masoncraft is much more agreeable than modern concrete, in their audacity, even stark-

124 WELLS: Strainer arches under the crossing, looking north

ness, they carry analogies with certain contemporary structures, especially bridges, in that material. Accordingly there are those who wax enthusiastic about the strainer arches of Wells; but the plain truth can only be that in a building so exquisitely detailed, so abounding in subtleties, they are a grotesque intrusion.

The third cathedral for which the first half of the fourteenth century was a period of capital importance is York. The rebuilding of the old Norman cathedral proceeded very slowly. The transepts have already been described. The Decorated portions are the chapter-house, the nave and the west front.

Ills. 73, 125 The chapter-house is one of the finest parts of the Minster. It was begun shortly after that at Southwell (which at the time was in the York diocese), but it took longer to complete. These two differ from all the other polygonal chapter-houses in dispensing with a central pier. At Southwell this was possible because, although the vault is of stone, the scale is small. At York the building is lofty and spacious, with an internal diameter of 58 ft, but, although the external buttresses make it certain that a vault was intended, it was never erected. The pretty star-shaped roof, finished in 1342, is only of wood imitating stone. More memorable are the windows, both in the chapter-house itself and in the lofty right-angled vestibule which gives access from the north transept. The traceries are not yet Flowing, but they are Geometrical at its most handsome. Moreover, they retain a good deal of their original early-fourteenth-century glass: the vestibule windows are among York's best.

Below the windows, however, with their formal, geometrical patterns, is a feature which seems to be imbued with a very different spirit: the overhanging canopies of the stalls. These canopies run round, in and out, in and out, in a ceaseless ripple, with a quantity of surface complication which is very typical of the developed Decorated style. Capitals, bosses and pendants are profusely adorned with small carvings – human heads, animals and plenty of foliage – of a broadly naturalistic kind which, although not the equal of Southwell and by no means free from restoration, can still provide both pleasure and, in the case of some of the animal carvings, moments of lively amusement. Above the stalls runs a band of leaves, and above that a feature found in no other chapter-house, a gallery at the base of the windows, with room for six more seats in each bay.

The nave furnishes another example of a new structure surrounding an older one; the west end of the Norman nave is indicated on *P. 276* the plan. The new one was a little wider and about two and a half bays longer. Although begun in 1291 it took over half a century to complete; at one point we are told that 'a long strike paralysed the work', which seems to have a very contemporary ring about it. This *Ill. 128* nave is the most imposing example of the Decorated style in

125 YORK: The chapter-house

England, but not the loveliest. The primary defect, once again, resides in the proportions. With an internal height of 93 ft – second only, among England's mediaeval churches, to Westminster Abbey – it might have been supposed that there would be no problem; but the builders seem to have felt that the size of the crossing in Archbishop de Gray's thirteenth-century transept demanded a breadth between the nave piers of as much as 48 ft. As a result, York nave is yet another English Gothic building which is too broad for its height. There can be no doubt that this defect was soon realized, for when the time came to rebuild the choir the proportions were altered and considerably improved.

In other ways, too, this nave can be seen to fall short of the highest standards of its brilliant period. Except at the west end, most of the window tracery, still Geometrical, is rather dull and monotonous. *Ill. 126* The clustered piers are lofty but their profile, with twelve shafts of varying thickness, is curiously insensitive, while their capitals, *Ill. 127* although not without charm when closely examined, are too small

126 *left.* YORK: Looking across the nave

127 *above.* YORK: Capital in the nave

128 YORK: The nave, looking west

129 YORK: The west front

and too tightly packed to be effective from below. Finally, there is the irony of exceptionally robust vaulting shafts rising in an unbroken sweep from the floor to support no more than a wooden roof imitating the stone vault which was intended. (The present roof is only a copy of the original, destroyed by fire in 1840.)

Yet when all has been said in criticism, the majesty of York remains unassailable. It was England's largest mediaeval church, a giant among the cathedrals, and the interior, if not perhaps very lovable, has great dignity and a fine spaciousness. The stained glass, although by the standards of the Middle Ages it seldom rises above medium quality, is nevertheless much superior to almost all Victorian and modern glass, and survives in such quantity that this cathedral interior glows and sparkles like no other in the country. That England never adopted the frequent continental practice of throwing out a succession of lateral chapels between the buttresses was very fortunate, for had this happened York would have lost both its large aisle windows and the ornamental arcade which, as at Durham, Lincoln and elsewhere, flows along below them as a delightful embellishment. Aloft, the sensation of verticality is enhanced by the treatment of the triforium and clerestory as a single unit: the mullions of the windows are carried straight down, and there is no passage at either level within the church; instead, a passage runs along outside the clerestory windows. This complete merging of clerestory and triforium was at this time a novelty in England, deriving certainly from France; it could be seen at Troyes, for example, before the end of the thirteenth century, and elsewhere soon after. Although its proportions may seem to belie the fact, the nave of York was undoubtedly more French in character than any other building in England since the choir of Canterbury, with the exception of Westminster Abbey.

The west front – completed, apart from the towers, by 1345 – is *Ill. 129* one of the Minster's most striking features. The boldly projecting buttresses, as at Wells, cast congenial shadows, and make a notable contribution to the general impression of strength and assurance. The doorways, although still small by French standards and ill provided with sculpture, have more scale and dignity than is usual in England. The big central window, particularly magnificent from within, was glazed in 1338. It is one of the most remarkable examples of Flowing tracery, and a precursor, one would say, of Flamboyant Gothic in France; its ingenious design embodies a sacred heart.

By now a picture should have emerged of the Decorated as a luxuriant style, often using forms ornamentally rather than structurally: hence the undulating surfaces, the elaboration of the window tracery, the proliferation of ribs and bosses at the vaults. This phase of English cathedral architecture was a gorgeous one in the exact meaning of the word: that is to say, 'adorned with rich or brilliant colours, showy, magnificent'. The colours and the gilding must never be forgotten. From about the middle of the thirteenth century, following the example set by Westminster Abbey, it seems certain that carved members, including not only figures but capitals and even mouldings, were often brightly coloured, and that in some places coloured patterns, especially diapers, would also be added. Much of the ironwork, screens and door-hinges for example, would be gilded as a matter of course. To modern eyes much of the applied colour and gilding might well have looked garish; on the other hand, it is undeniable that carved members such as bosses, only visible from a distance, are far more effective when coloured.

Decorated art can be shallow and superficial, although even then it usually manages at least to be pretty. But in many buildings, mostly cathedrals, this stands revealed as a period bold in spatial adventure, daring in structural achievement, sumptuous in ornamental enrichment. Some of the other outstanding works will now be briefly described.

By 1300 little remained to be done at Lincoln except to carry up the towers. But early in the fourteenth century two other glorious *Ill. 130* additions were made. One was the pulpitum or choir screen. It would not be possible to find a better illustration of the magnificence of Decorated art at its best. To either side of the central opening are four tall ogee-headed niches, separated by buttresses most exquisitely fashioned, with triplets of tiny gables at three different levels, and diapers above and below. Diapers in the form of much larger rosettes adorn the niches, too, while in the mouldings of the arches there are flowers, leaves and little animals. Behind the arches it will be found that each niche has its own delicious little ribbed vault. The whole of this screen was undoubtedly coloured, and indeed traces of the original colouring still remain. One other English cathedral,

130 LINCOLN: Part of the pulpitum, west side

Southwell, which is only twenty-three miles from Lincoln, has a smaller screen of comparable splendour and of much the same date.

About the same time (*c.* 1325) the end-wall of the south transept was reconstructed. For some reason rose-windows never enjoyed much popularity in mediaeval England. Westminster Abbey had two fine examples in the transepts – not the two one sees today – and about 1300 St Paul's Cathedral in London was given a new east end that culminated in seven tall lancets surmounted by the most splendid rose in the country, some 40 ft across. But these were exceptions, and among the few others of any size were the two, both with plate-tracery, at the ends of the great transepts at Lincoln. In the north transept the original rose ('the Dean's Eye') still survives, but opposite, with splendid extravagance, the early-thirteenth-century rose was removed and replaced by a circular window as *Ill. 131* unusual as it is successful. The bar-tracery of 'the Bishop's Eye' recalls two immense leaves, and the window is framed by an arch comprising a double row of pierced quatrefoils. Today it shimmers with gorgeous colour, yet apart from a single figure the glass consists only of fragments, of many different dates. How little it matters: the beauty of the material is its own justification. Perhaps there is no branch of art in which the quality of the material itself counts for more than with stained glass. Here, certainly, the tracery itself plays the theme; the glass is only the accompaniment, and since it is but a collection of fragments it could not be otherwise. But with tracery like this there can be no room for regrets.

The central tower built about 1200 collapsed some forty years later. The lower part of the present tower is Early English work of about 1250, and was crowned with a wooden spire covered with lead. Hardly more than fifty years later the chapter determined to remove this spire and raise the height of the tower in the most sumptuous style. It was all accomplished in five years (1306–1311), and on top of this arose the prodigiously high spire, destroyed in 1548, to which reference was made on page 26. When the two west towers were carried up is not known, but it would seem to have been about 1400. They also had their wooden spires, as shown in *Ill. 133* Joseph Baker's painting of 1742; these were removed in 1807. The

131 LINCOLN: The south transept, with the 'Bishop's Eye'

132 *left*. LINCOLN: Central tower vault

133 *below*. LINCOLN: Painting by Joseph Baker (1742) showing wooden spires

Ills. 134, 8 three towers make a famous and wonderful group, visible for miles. They illustrate what is known as the polygonal corner-buttress type of tower at its most remarkable. On the west towers the size of these buttresses, fixed by the Normans, is excessive. Although an impression of great strength is conveyed, the intervening walls and windows seem somewhat crushed by these huge corner-buttresses. By contrast the buttresses of the central tower are perfectly proportioned. The Decorated part, the belfry, consists of a single stage, with a pair of very lofty gabled windows, each of two lights, on every face. Their frames are delightfully ornamented with crockets and ball-flower. The pierced parapets and lead-covered pinnacles are as late as the third quarter of the eighteenth century, but they are very successful. The western pair are more than 200 ft high, and the central one reaches 271 ft, which makes it easily the loftiest mediaeval tower in England. It is also one of the loveliest, within no less than without. This is a lantern tower and incorporates a fascinating *Ill. 132* lierne-vault, probably added towards the end of the fourteenth century.

Whereas in the fifteenth century towers were sometimes designed from the outset to be no more than towers, in the Decorated period

134 LINCOLN: View from the south-west

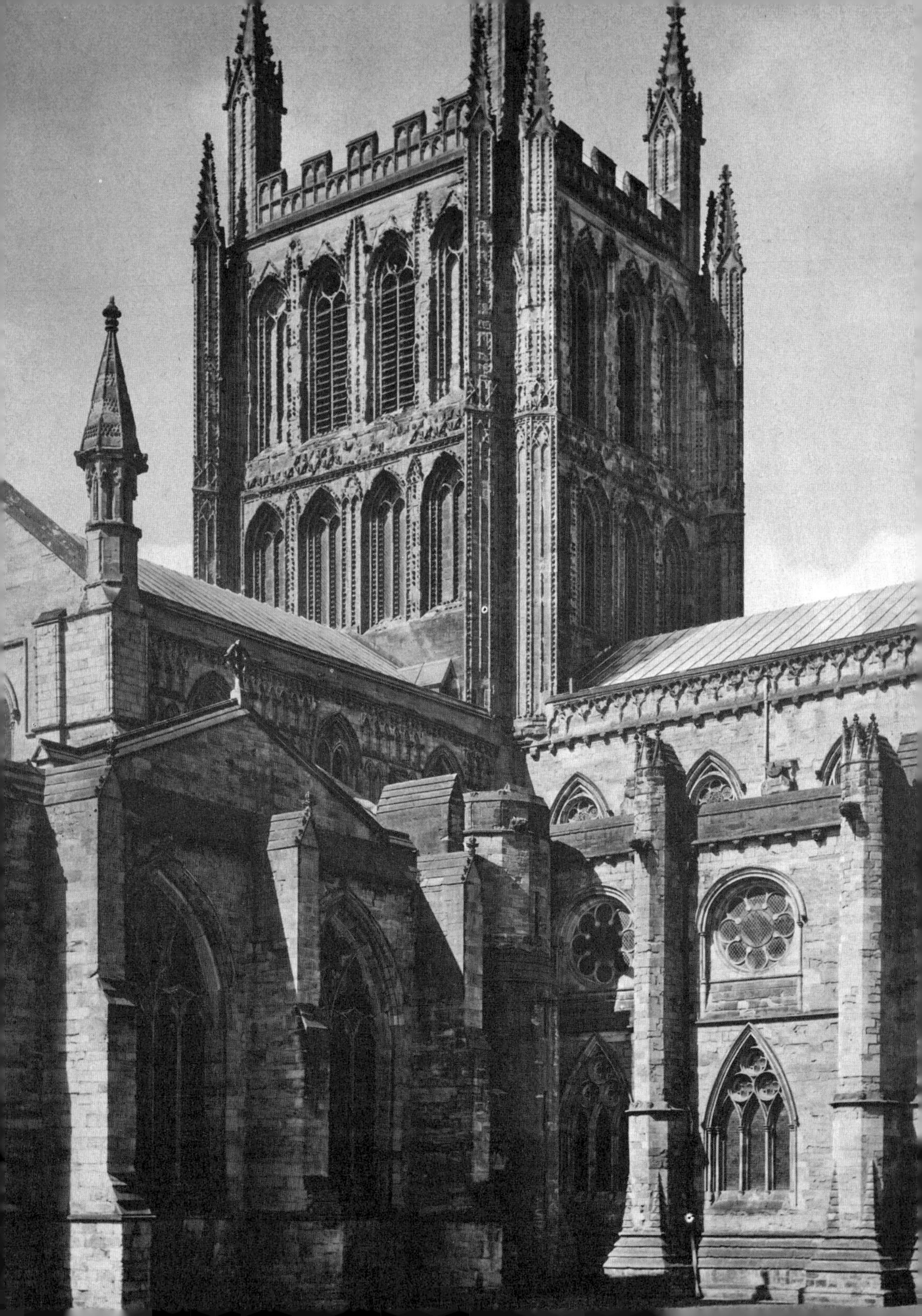

they always culminated in spires, even though these might only be of wood. Hereford was no exception; the lead-covered timber spire survived there until 1790, and it was not until forty years later that the large corner-pinnacles were added. This tower is not very high, *Ill. 135* but is at once so massive and so gorgeous that the loss of the spire does not seem to matter. The buttresses are like Siamese twins, and project diagonally from the corners. This arrangement, though somewhat complicated, is very successful, and the clustered pinnacles are delightful. There are no less than eight two-light windows, pierced or blind, on each face, while the ball-flower ornamentation is among the most exuberant in the country. Unfortunately the sandstone masonry of this grand tower is now in a state of decay.

At Salisbury, after the completion of the cloisters and chapter-house about 1284, there was a pause. For almost exactly fifty years the builders held their breath, as it were, before making their final and supreme effort. Then they started on the upper stages of the tower, and the spire, which seems to grow out of it so inevitably, *Ills. 7, 67* followed at once. Although in its scale and silhouette the tower has a good deal in common with Lincoln, in details, both of composition and ornamentation, it is much closer to Hereford. Again we find eight two-light windows, in two tiers and some of them blind, on each face. Again the surface is studded with ball-flower, in the utmost profusion, and a ball-flower moulding is carried up each of the eight ridges of the spire. Horizontally, the spire is embellished with three carved ornamental bands at carefully judged intervals; otherwise the surface is completely plain, and rightly so. Best of all is the way in which the transition from the square to the octagon was achieved, a problem to which mediaeval builders devoted much thought and plenty of experimentation. Here there are a double tier of pinnacles at each corner and a gabled spire-light, or lucarne, at a lower level in between: a perfect solution. The spire of Salisbury, 404 ft high, is loftier by nearly a hundred feet than any other in England; but it is not so much for its great height as for its exquisite grace that one may claim for it the supreme place among spires – of any date and in any land. One does not lightly employ the word faultless, but here, for once, it seems to be the *mot juste*.

135 HEREFORD: The central tower

A unique and arresting achievement of the Late Decorated period is the octagon at Ely. The original central tower, built just before 1100, fell in 1322. On the initiative of Alan of Walsingham, the sacrist in charge of works and later prior of the monastery, the opportunity was taken to widen considerably the space at the crossing and, with great daring on the part both of the master-mason and of the master-carpenter, to erect what might be described as the Gothic equivalent of the Classical dome. The octagon is of stone, but the lantern which rises above its centre is of wood, faced externally with lead. For the vertical members eight giant oak beams, each about 63 ft long and 3 ft 4 in. thick at the lower end, were brought from Chicksands in Bedfordshire. The lantern had to be wholly renewed by George Gilbert Scott, but it is said that the original design was carefully copied. *Ill. 136*

Internally the octagon provides one of the wonders of English cathedral architecture, marred only by the windows in the diagonal walls, which have over-complicated, unattractive tracery and some particularly poor Victorian glass. Looking up, most of what we see, it is true, is of wood – the lovely vault with its tierceron ribs and the whole of the lantern. Purists have accordingly been heard to complain that, given the material, it was a mistake to evolve what is essentially a lithic design. In stone it would doubtless have been still more satisfying, but with a diameter of about 69 ft a stone vault was a structural impossibility. As a feat of construction, even the wooden substitute was a remarkable achievement; the massive vertical posts of the lantern were supported on hammer-beams, introduced here a few years earlier than in the Pilgrims' Hall at Winchester, which is said to have the earliest known hammer-beam roof. (To see these it is necessary to climb up behind the wooden vaulting.) Aesthetically, the chief delights of the octagon are a sudden sensation of space for which the long Norman nave has left us quite unprepared, and especially, when looking up, the contrast between the shadowy vaulting of the wider area and the bright light flooding on to the eight-pointed star of the octagon. *Ills. 137–139*

136 ELY: The Octagon, from the west tower

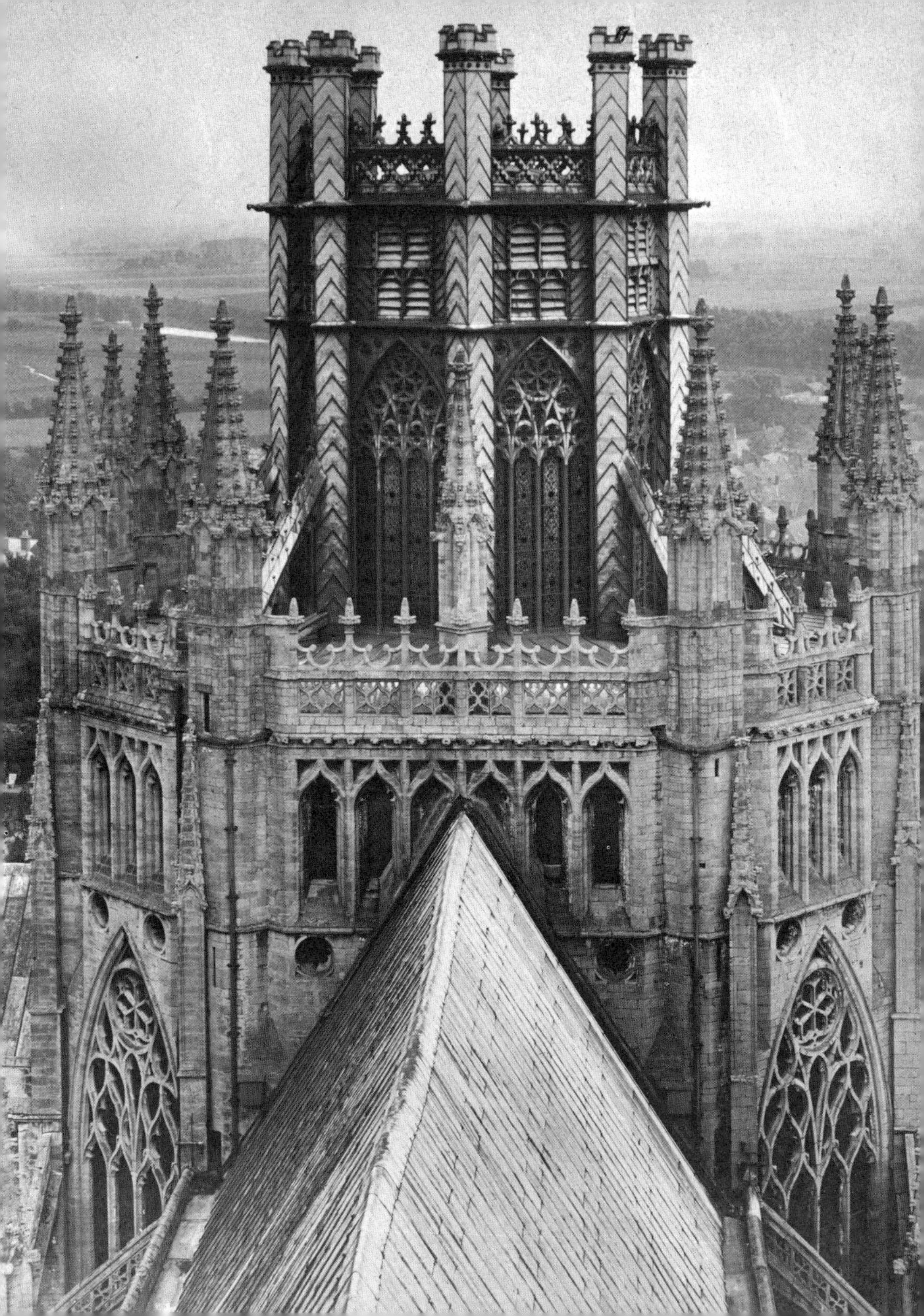

137 ELY: The Octagon.

138 ELY: The Octagon, looking west towards the nave

139 ELY: The Octagon, looking north-west

The Lady Chapel at Ely is not in the usual situation at the east end, but to the north-east of the north transept, almost detached from the cathedral itself. It was begun in 1321, but the fall of the tower in the following year caused a long interruption, and the peculiar east window, an unhappy example of Gothic ingenuity, was not completed until 1373. It is England's largest Lady Chapel, and has the widest mediaeval vault in the country, with a span of 46 ft. (The vault of York nave would have been 2 ft wider had it been built.) The interior was once a blaze of colour, and its sculptural embellishment very elaborate. But the carvings represented the life-story of

Ill. 77

Ill. 141

140 ELY: The Lady Chapel. Detail of arcade

141 ELY: The Lady Chapel. Interior looking west

the Virgin Mary, a subject which inevitably aroused the particular wrath of the Protestants at the time of the Reformation, so the damage was punitive. Only the foliage carving was spared, and this, which is in clunch, is rather too reminiscent of a parsley-bed. Today, with the stained glass and painted details all but gone, the principal interest centres on the design of the arcade below the windows. This shows Decorated at its most sophisticated. Above each niche the head of the arch bends forward, to form what is known as a nodding ogee. Repeated all round the chapel, this has the effect of imparting to the wall-surface a kind of plasticity of which the stall-canopies in the York chapter-house are the forerunners. Here, in fact, the ripple has gathered both strength and momentum.

Ill. 140

142 NORWICH:
The Prior's door

The figure sculpture of the later Decorated period is notable above all for its grace. Often the people are seen in swaying poses, and generally in exuberant settings. An unusual composition of great *Ill. 142* charm is the Prior's door into the cloisters at Norwich, dating from about 1310. The seven little figures in the arch include a seated Christ between angels, a pope, and John the Baptist in a camel-hair robe (on the left). Behind them are gables, the alternate ones of ogee form, with a profusion of crockets. The radial arrangement is the special feature here; it is delightful. At Rochester, dating from a few years later, the disposition is more traditional but the sculpture itself

143 ROCHESTER:
Doorway to the chapter-room

is more accomplished. The doorway illustrated is in the south transept and now gives access to the chapter-room. The standing figures, clad in thin, clinging robes, are the Church and the Synagogue, a subject which had been treated so memorably in France at Rheims, Strasbourg and elsewhere; both heads here have had to be renewed. Above them, seated at their desks, are the Four Evangelists (or perhaps Doctors of the Church), and at the apex a human soul – presumably that of the donor – being rescued by angels from Purgatory. The frame suffers from restoration, but the spirit of Decorated art has not been lost. *Ill. 143*

Of the great display of Decorated sculpture on the west front of Lichfield virtually nothing survives. All the statues, except five high up on the north-west tower, are Victorian, and might pass as an advertisement for the local hairdresser, every little wisp of hair on every figure having been carefully 'set' in a fussy little curl. From the sculpture, therefore, our attention turns to the architecture. Although now largely a reproduction – the window is barely a century old – the design of the original front can still be appreciated. Started about 1280, it was complete by 1327 apart from the spires, which were not begun until the closing years of the fourteenth century. In its silhouette the west front of Lichfield is closer to a typical French façade than any other in England; but in the ordering of its parts it is very different, for it turns out to be yet another example of the screen type of front. The horizontal disposition is clear and good: the tiers of figures under canopies are even carried round the octagonal corner-turrets. The vertical articulation on the other hand, in contrast to Wells, is very weak: about half-way down, the towers lose their identity altogether. Other English characteristics include the smallness of the doors, the bringing forward of the gable flush with the rest of the front, and the excessive flatness, which is interrupted by certain openings inwards but hardly at all by anything in the way of an outward projection that would cast a shadow. Thus when on a summer evening all the doors are open and jet-black shadows are revealed beyond, this front is greatly improved; it acquires a depth, a third dimension, which it badly needs.

Ill. 144

Lichfield is most admired today for its three stone spires, the Ladies of the Vale. The central spire had to be completely rebuilt in the 1660s after the Civil War, and the western spires have also been reconstructed, but the trio was envisaged in the Decorated period and still has considerable charm. The air photograph also shows, at the east end of the cathedral, the Lady Chapel, built between about 1320 and 1336. This is a stately and for England a most unusual addition, for although the pitch of the roof is flatter it rises internally to the full height (57 ft) of the cathedral. Being aisleless, it is in effect a lofty hall; the extremely tall traceried windows without transoms

Ill. 145

144 LICHFIELD: The west front

are of a type not uncommon in French churches of this period but
Ill. 146 almost without parallel north of the Channel. French also is the
Ill. 81 polygonal east end which provides a noble termination to the interior. The seven easternmost windows are adorned with early-sixteenth-century glass from the Abbey of Herkenrode in Belgium, acquired by purchase in 1802.

The proliferation of Lady Chapels in the later thirteenth and early fourteenth centuries was a reflection of the cult of the Virgin Mary mentioned earlier. Only when, as at Southwell, a whole church was dedicated to the Virgin was a Lady Chapel considered unnecessary. It was originally intended that the Lichfield Lady Chapel, like that at Wells, should be detached from the main building; the existing presbytery, linking the chapel to the choir, was a slightly later addition, and a very skilful one, because choir and chapel are not on the same axis. The reason was not symbolic (a great deal of nonsense has been talked about the alleged symbolism of 'weeping'

145 LICHFIELD: Air view, from the north-west

146 LICHFIELD: The Lady Chapel

chancels) but structural. Lichfield Cathedral is built upon a natural bed of sandstone, which veers towards the north-east. What the ingenious architect did was to modify the axis of the presbytery from one bay to the next.

An aisleless hall in England was sufficiently remarkable, but during these same years the Augustinian canons of Bristol were building something unique among the English cathedrals, a *Hallenkirche* or hall-church: a church with side aisles rising as high as the centre. The achievement is the more remarkable in that there was very little money, so little in fact that they are recorded as having to beg for food from the citizens or go hungry. Externally, it must be admitted, Bristol Cathedral, heavy and smoke-begrimed, is not inspiring. The original nave was destroyed in the sixteenth century and the present one, by Street, was finished only in 1888. He was also responsible for the west towers, while the central tower was rebuilt by Pearson in the 1890s. But internally the eastern part of this cathedral is one of the most original creations of the Middle Ages. As so often in the

German hall-churches, the absence of clerestory windows renders the vault of the central area (one of the first of the lierne type) somewhat dark. The aisles, on the other hand, are well lit by tall traceried windows, and their loftiness offered the designer the opportunity of

Ill. 147 working out an extremely ingenious scheme of vaulting. The thrust of the central vault is transferred to the external buttresses by means of a series of horizontal struts across the aisles, carried upon transverse arches with pierced spandrels. Every aisle bay is then given a small ribbed vault of its own, partly springing from the centre of each strut. The fascination of this design is beyond question. Whether it can really be called beautiful seems to me more doubtful. But it is illuminating to find Nikolaus Pevsner, with his European viewpoint, observing that 'the work at Bristol from the point of view of spatial imagination is superior to anything else built in England and indeed in Europe at the same time. It proves incontrovertibly that English design surpassed that of all other countries during the first third of the fourteenth century.'[9]

147 BRISTOL: South choir aisle, looking east

148 CARLISLE: The choir, looking east

Little has yet been said in this book of Carlisle. A cathedral church since 1133, it has been one of England's unluckiest, having to cope not only with a friable stone and, in 1292, a very bad fire, but also with specially ruthless handling at the time of the Civil War, when the Parliamentarians tore down most of the nave because they wanted stone for fortifications; it has never been rebuilt. Carlisle preserves one show-piece, however: its east window, the largest example of Flowing Decorated in England (51 ft high and 26 ft broad), and one of the last; it was certainly incomplete, perhaps hardly begun, at the time of the Black Death. Except in some of the tracery lights, the original glass has unfortunately been destroyed. But this window has often been described, for its tracery, as the finest in the kingdom. Like the Bristol vaults, it is a *tour de force*: it is said that on the drawing-board the designer had to strike his tracery from two hundred and sixty-three different centres. It has a rich complexity which is fascinating to follow through in detail, and needless to say it provides a glorious termination to the choir. Yet for sheer loveliness of Late Decorated design those who know the rather smaller east window of Selby Abbey in Yorkshire may hesitate to award to Carlisle the palm.

Ill. 148

CHAPTER EIGHT

Perpendicular

THERE HAVE BEEN two notable phases in her long architectural history when England has reacted decisively against contemporary developments on the continent of Europe. On both occasions the English move was in the direction of more discipline and greater sobriety. In early Georgian days, while continental countries were sunning themselves in the exuberance of the High Baroque and preparing to embrace the still wilder fancies of the Rococo, the English landed class, with Lord Burlington as their architectural leader, veered back to the strictest and most formal Classicism. Nearly four hundred years earlier, the pendulum of English Gothic also swung decisively back, renouncing the convolutions of the Flamboyant in favour of a very different mode of architectural expression, one that had no parallel elsewhere.

It has been said that later Gothic architecture in England is lacking in warmth. It is undeniable that in this period the general effect is usually better than the details, which can look mechanical – what has been termed 'businessman's Gothic'. A single motif will be repeated from bay to bay with unvarying precision, as in Classical architecture. But in scale these buildings are sometimes magnificent, in craftsmanship superb; and at its best this architecture attains a stateliness, even a nobility, that makes a really powerful appeal.

Although England was now growing richer, and more money than ever was flowing into the coffers of the Church, cathedral foundations were no longer the principal beneficiaries. At Canterbury the shrine of St Thomas was still much visited. At Winchester that remarkable man William of Wykeham (1324–1404), who started life as a village boy and at forty-three had become Chancellor of England, paid for much of the reconstruction out of his own very ample resources. But no more cathedrals were founded during this time, and very regrettably there is not a single one which is wholly

149 GLOUCESTER: The choir, looking east

in the Perpendicular style. The nearest approach to a cathedral is Bath Abbey, which is wholly Perpendicular, but a very late example.

Monastic foundations received still less, because for various reasons the monks were now unpopular. Thus when in this period abbey and priory churches received new buildings or fresh embellishments – and a fair number did – it was usually because they were able to meet the cost from large existing revenues or from some special cause, of which the outstanding example is the Abbey (not yet cathedral) of Gloucester. Here the Abbot, with great acumen, acquired in 1330 not merely the remains of a king, but of a *murdered* king: Edward II. His horrible death practically turned him into a saint or martyr, and his relics into miracle-workers. Pilgrimages to his shrine were soon bringing to Gloucester an enormous access of wealth, and it was not long before an ambitious rebuilding programme was put in hand. It is now generally held that the Perpendicular style was first evolved in 1330–1331, not, as used to be said, at Gloucester, but in London, in St Stephen's chapel at Westminster and in the chapter-house of Old St Paul's, both long since the victims of fire; but the earliest work at Gloucester followed almost immediately. Thereafter rebuilding was carried on more or less continuously for about a hundred and fifty years. The Norman plan
Ill. 155 can still easily be recognized, but except for the nave, the whole of the old Benedictine abbey church was either remodelled or rebuilt in the Perpendicular period. Among the cathedrals, therefore, Gloucester is the archetype of the style.

Work on the south transept started in 1331 and reached the eleventh-century choir six years later; the remodelling took about twenty years to complete. The original choir design was quite
Ill. 150 different from that of the nave. There was an unusually low arcade, and a large tribune borne on very massive circular piers. Those piers remain. Only on the sides facing the choir itself were they pared down and given a 'new look'. Yet spatially both the aisles and the tribunes were now pushed out into the cold. A cage of stonework was introduced, the intention of which could only have been to mask the Norman work, and this cage was extended upwards to embrace an entirely new clerestory of huge dimensions.

150 GLOUCESTER: The choir, looking north-east

Looking at the photograph, it is easy to recognize why some people dislike the term Perpendicular. Certainly, the slender vaulting shafts soar upwards in an unbroken sweep, but so they do in a number of earlier buildings, even some very early ones like Ely, Peterborough and Durham. The downward extension of the mullions of the clerestory windows to produce additional vertical lines is much more novel, and these are undeniably 'perpendicular'. But the most striking innovation is not the greater employment of verticals but the introduction of horizontals – the cross-pieces or transoms. Originating from the need to strengthen the mullions of windows which were now growing ever larger, this feature soon appeared where there were no windows, as here in front of the tribune, and elsewhere to help to panel blank wall-surfaces. Rectilinear would therefore have been a better name than Perpendicular. However, the essential point to recognize is that it was the flowing curve which was now rejected.

By the banishment from sight of the Romanesque aisles and *Ill. 149* tribunes, the choir of Gloucester attains a striking architectural unity. It is so light and so cage-like that it has been compared to a gigantic greenhouse; but of course it is far more than that. Except at the vault, the details are no longer interesting. Gone are the finely carved capitals of some of the earlier cathedrals; gone too, with few exceptions, are such details as sculptured corbels and hood-mould terminals and rich wall arcades. The design reveals the utmost skill and the masoncraft is splendid, but a certain thinness, bloodlessness even, may also be detected. The stateliness is unquestionable, but the spirit is aloof.

The east window, 38 ft wide and 72 ft high, was constructed between 1347 and 1350 and still remains the largest stone-traceried window in England as regards the area of its glass, which is about the same as that of a lawn-tennis court. It has two features which were not repeated in other windows of this kind. It is not all in one plane: the side portions are canted somewhat, apparently to allow room for still more glass. And behind the thick mullions are a pair of quite considerable buttresses, which were soon found to be unnecessary. Otherwise this window, which still preserves much of its original glass, sparkling like icicles in the sunshine of a crisp winter's day, set a fashion which was followed during the next two centuries in window after window. The next big one, the very similar west *Ill. 151* window at Winchester of about 1360, came in for a scathing analysis from Ruskin (*Stones of Venice*, vol. 1, ch. 17), and I mention this because I believe most of his criticisms to be valid. He deplored the

151 WINCHESTER: The nave, looking west

large number of transoms; he objected to the mullions running straight up into the arch-head; he abominated what he called the 'carving-knife' shapes, seen at Gloucester in the canted parts to either side. He might have added that these enormous windows seldom look well when viewed externally. To improve the lighting they were wonderfully effective, but this was only achieved at some artistic cost. At Gloucester there is still a slight inflection at the point where the mullions strike the curve of the arch. Later there was usually none, and this always seems insensitive.

152, 153 GLOUCESTER: Part of the choir vault. The vault at the crossing

The vault is another early example of the lierne type, rather net-like in this instance. Some of the bosses are attractive, and a few are very large. The majority are foliated, but over the high altar there is a choir of fifteen angelic musicians (to accompany the *Gloria in Excelsis*), which are now wholly gilded. The carving, remembering that they are some 80 ft above the floor, is what it should be: bold rather than refined. They are among the best angel sculptures of the later Gothic Age. This vault continues westwards without interruption to the far, that is to say west, side of the central tower; thus it had to pass the openings into the transepts, to clear which its most westerly pair of segments hung too low. So an extraordinary expedient was devised: thin bridges were built across these openings to carry the vault segments. This was brilliantly ingenious; a typical example, in fact, of the Gloucester masons' virtuosity.

Ill. 152

Ill. 153

The transepts and choir were the great pioneer works; the Perpendicular style can also be seen at Gloucester in the tower and

154 GLOUCESTER: The Lady Chapel, looking west

cloisters (both of which will be discussed later), the not very distinguished west front, and the Lady Chapel. This last, although over a century later in date, is in many ways an echo of the choir, and a very charming one. There are no aisles, but the whole wall-surface is panelled, in either stone or glass, while many more bosses
Ill. 154 enrich the lierne-vault. The view westwards shows the low entrance bay with a gallery above, seen through a complex web of open tracery.

155 GLOUCESTER: Air view from the north-west

The three major undertakings of the second half of the fourteenth century, none finished until after 1400, were the nave of Canterbury, the nave of Winchester and the choir of York. The two former provide a fascinating comparison, for they enable us to watch the two leading English master-masons – or as we should say, architects – of the time, Henry Yevele at Canterbury and William Wynford at Winchester, facing the same problem: what to do about an imposing but antiquated and no doubt ill-lit Norman nave some three hundred years old. Yevele's solution was radical: take it down to the ground and start again. This he did, except only for the north-west tower, which survived until 1834, when it gave place to a copy of the south-west tower. (This is sometimes described as an act of vandalism, as archaeologically it was; but from the aesthetic standpoint there can be little doubt that the replacement of Lanfranc's old tower greatly improved the appearance of the cathedral.) The new nave was, however, no longer than the old, and with only nine bays is relatively short for England.

The 'stone girder' at the east end of Canterbury's nave is one of two which had to be inserted early in the sixteenth century when the central tower was rebuilt; it was a tactful and ingenious expedient but is none the less a pity. Otherwise there is virtually nothing to criticize. This is without doubt one of the most stately and one of the most elegant achievements of English architecture. The proportions are quite different from those of the Early Gothic cathedrals. *Ills. 156–158* The main arcade is now very lofty, whereas the clerestory windows are small and the triforium is no more than a downward extension, in panelled form, of the clerestory window-tracery, a device which has already been encountered in the nave of York. The principal light comes from the aisle windows, as in a hall-church, and there was a practical reason for the loftiness of these aisles: on the north side, one walk of the cloisters abuts on to the church wall. Windows could only therefore be introduced above the cloister roof. But although by comparison with, say, Westminster Abbey the internal proportions may seem a little strange, a wonderful sense of space was achieved at Canterbury without the sacrifice of clerestory lighting. The beautiful piers are relatively but not excessively slender; the horizontal lines are subordinate to the vertical; the shafts sweep up 80 ft from the floor to a simple but completely satisfying lierne-vault.

156 CANTERBURY: The nave, looking east

157 Canterbury: The nave, from the north aisle looking south-west

158 CANTERBURY: The nave, looking west

An airy spaciousness is of the essence of this lovely nave. That is what the designer was obviously seeking to achieve, and he succeeded completely. If, however, you cherish so much the weightiness and dignity of massive piers as to feel that the Canterbury nave is too light, too stylish one might almost say, then you will undoubtedly *Ill. 159* prefer Winchester. Here, although ingeniously transformed, the Norman core was mostly retained, and quite a different feeling results. The aisles at Winchester are much less prominent than at *Ill. 160* Canterbury. The arches of the main arcade are both lower and narrower, and the design of each bay, instead of being nearly all in one plane and strongly vertical in emphasis, is marked at the level of the triforium by a horizontal division in the form of a small panelled parapet borne on a frieze of carved corbels. The clerestory windows are considerably recessed. The point of springing of the vault ribs is also several feet lower than at Canterbury, but the pitch of the vault is so much steeper that at the ridge there is a difference of only 2 ft between them. The Winchester vault is again of the lierne type, but although it looks much more complex than Canterbury's, the pattern is easily grasped, and there are far larger and finer bosses. It is unfortunate that Gilbert Scott's choir screen, like the fine early-fourteenth-century canopied stalls on which it was modelled, is so black as to be quite out of tone with the silver-grey stonework. A more restful and less spiky design for the screen would also have been much better. Between 1638 and 1820 this cathedral had a

159 WINCHESTER: Elevation, showing transformation of Norman work

160 WINCHESTER: The interior, looking east

classical screen in stone by Inigo Jones, parts of which survive at Winchester itself and in a museum at Cambridge.[10]

Winchester has the advantage over Canterbury of greater length, for here the Norman nave had twelve bays; yet one can imagine a Frenchman, with mind and eye attuned to those concentrated spatial effects referred to earlier (p. 88), not regarding this as advantageous, but holding rather that so much length only served to render it more tunnel-like. I should be very reluctant to agree; the huge piers endow Winchester's interior with a slow rhythm of great majesty which, for all the differences in ornamental enrichment, link it spiritually with Durham. Canterbury, on the contrary, looks forward to King's College Chapel at Cambridge. Which is the finer, Winchester or Canterbury, is indeed difficult to determine; each in its own way is a masterpiece.

At York it was the choir of the Norman church which still remained in 1360, and for some time it had been proving inadequate. There was also no Lady Chapel. The following year, therefore, saw the launching of another ambitious rebuilding project, embracing the choir, the presbytery with short but lofty eastern transepts, and the retro-choir which, although of the same dimensions as the rest,

161 YORK: Air view from the south-east

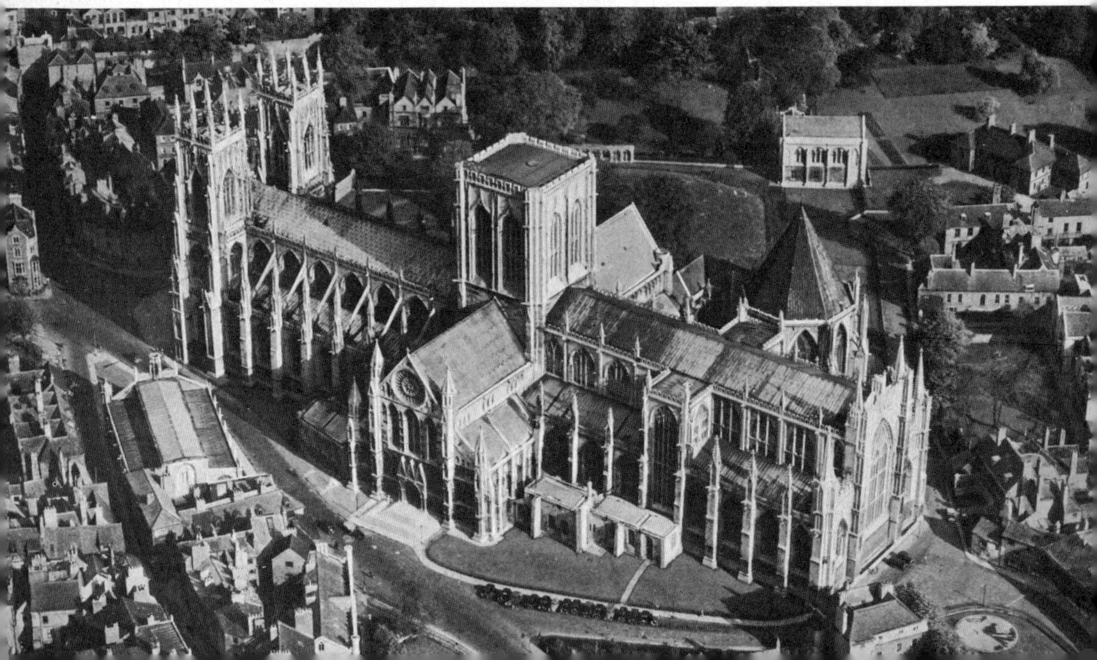

162 YORK: The choir, looking east

was to be used as a Lady Chapel. In its leading features this part of the Minster follows fairly closely the design of the nave, with the result that among English mediaeval cathedrals only Salisbury and Exeter achieve a greater degree of stylistic unity than York. But partly perhaps for the very reason that the nave provided the model, this choir falls a long way short of the naves of Canterbury and Winchester as a work of art. It is an improvement on the nave, the piers being somewhat bolder, the capitals larger. But neither of the two triforium designs in the eastern limb is any more pleasing than that of the nave; the window-tracery is no better; the roof is again only of wood imitating stone, a copy of the original one burnt by a madman in 1829. It has great dignity, and some beautiful stained glass, yet it is curiously staid and earthbound. The east window is surpassed in size only by that at Gloucester and, in the present century, Liverpool, but the design leaves a good deal to be desired. Altogether there are 117 panels, arranged in thirteen rows of nine

Ill. 162

163 York: The east end

each, and 144 compartments in the tracery. The curious little gallery which runs across the centre of the window and involves the duplication of the mullions in the lower half is no asset here; it makes for confusion. But the glass, better preserved and with much less white than at Gloucester, is a splendid addition. This window was glazed by John Thornton of Coventry between 1405 and 1408.

Externally the most striking characteristic of York Minster is its sheer bulk. Although it lacks poetry, it conveys a great impression of size. The cliff-like east end is a success. The panelling round the window and on the flanking buttresses is typical of the age. More unexpected is the array of spirelets, and especially the outer pair, surmounting octagonal turrets which have buttresses that project at the four cardinal points, a charming idea. *Ill. 163*

The Perpendicular period, however unimaginative it may have been in its window design and, with rare exceptions, in its sculpture, was a grand time for tower building, and still to some extent for spires too. A number of English cathedrals now saw the completion of their long-projected towers or the heightening of existing ones. Structurally these great towers set tremendous problems for their builders, but visually they are of the first importance, for it is to its towers, far more than to any other single feature, that a cathedral owes its characteristic image.

The central tower of York (at the time of writing, a source of substantial anxiety) sums up to perfection the character of that cathedral. It was built during the first quarter of the fifteenth century, immediately following the completion of the choir. It is the largest in England in floor area, and – at a height of 180 ft – stone-vaulted, which was not the usual practice at York. But externally for all its massive dignity it is, again, staid: very impressive in scale, it yet lacks radiance. The lofty pairs of windows are sedate and the battlements might almost be called prim. The omission for reasons of safety of the projected corner-pinnacles was artistically a misfortune, for they could have provided just that touch of aspiration which is lacking. *Ills. 73, 161*

Ill. 164 The earliest of the Perpendicular cathedral towers is Worcester, finished in 1374. At that time it carried a lead-covered timber spire, the disappearance of which may be regarded as no loss. Close to, one cannot fail to be aware how grievously this tower has suffered from later refacing. Yet the design is beautiful, the proportions exquisite. The strong corner-buttresses are admirably managed and the crown, with its lofty crocketed pinnacles, is very handsome.

Although not built until about eighty years later, the magnificent *Ill. 165* tower at Gloucester clearly derives from Worcester. It is loftier – 225 ft as against 196 ft – and built of a much better stone. It has been criticized, and with some justice, for the handling of its surface decoration, which for all its exuberance is not free from monotony,

164 WORCESTER: View from the north-west

165 GLOUCESTER: The tower from the south-west

and also for the too pronounced character of its horizontal divisions, for which the bold string-courses carried over the buttresses are mainly responsible. That these latter are set diagonally to each wall-face is very unusual for a big tower. But the general proportions are extremely fine, and the sumptuous coronal is a delight. This consists of a very lofty parapet, pierced and battlemented, and at the corners four tall turrets, similarly pierced, which echo in miniature the design of the tower itself. These culminate in open spirelets, and needless to say no larger spire was ever envisaged here.

In the meantime, some notable tower building had been going on at Wells. Starting in 1365, first the south-west and then the north-west towers were carried up; together these took seventy years to
Ill. 166 complete. After that it was time to turn back to the central tower, which thanks to its big inverted arches had now stood for a century without showing any further signs of settlement. This tower had attained its present height as early as 1321, but originally it seems only to have had four corner-pinnacles and three pairs of long thin lancets on each face. The Perpendicular alterations were carried out about 1440. Within the cathedral the base of the tower was given a fine fan-vault. Outside, the long thin lancets were shortened and subdivided horizontally. But the principal changes were at the top: traceried parapets were introduced, together with no less than twenty subsidiary pinnacles, three grouped round the main pinnacle at each angle and two more crowning the sub-buttresses on each face. In addition, high up on the large corner-buttresses stand eight statues in canopied recesses. It is a glorious crown to a tower which, although not very lofty (182 ft), is so gracious, so harmonious in its proportions that very few can rival it. (It should perhaps be added that one of the best views, from the south-east, has been half-spoiled by a graveyard with horrible memorials in white marble and pink granite which one would like to see abolished as soon as possible. Wells, a delightful verger once said to me, after I had raised an eyebrow at the sight of a couple of itinerant dogs sniffing round the high altar, is almost too tolerant. 'When I was a young man at the Theological College,' he added, 'I was told that there was only one rule here: no smoking in the cathedral on Fridays!')

166 Wells: View from the south-east

At Durham during a severe storm in 1429 the old central tower was struck by lightning and caught fire. Little is known about this tower, but it was probably not very high. Rebuilding began about 1465 and continued for twenty-five years, but in two bounds *Ill. 168* separated by a short interval. The great weakness of this design is that the upper stage, which should be the tallest, looks like an afterthought: and so it was. Just below the upper windows run battlements which were obviously designed to be the crown of the 1465 tower. It seems a pity that they were not taken off and perhaps reused higher up. Nevertheless, this massive tower adds strength to the exterior of the cathedral at exactly the point where it was most *Ill. 167* needed. It is, moreover, apparent from the distant view that in relation to the western towers (144 ft) the decision to raise its height to 218 ft was artistically right.

We have reached 1490, with a Tudor now on the throne; but the supreme masterpiece of Perpendicular tower building was still to *Ill. 169* come. Bell Harry, the central tower of Canterbury, 235 ft high, was

168 DURHAM: The central tower

167 DURHAM: View across the city from the north-west

built between 1494 and 1497. The architect was one of England's greatest: John Wastell, whom we shall shortly be meeting again. In design it is markedly original, with no close resemblance to any other tower. Its dominant characteristics are its slender, graceful form and its unhesitating verticality to which its angle-buttresses, bold, complex and untapering, contribute not a little. The beautiful and highly individual corner-pinnacles were inspired by those already in existence on the south-west tower. A little-known structural feature of Bell Harry, very unusual for its date, is that it is lined with red bricks, said to number 480,000. The facing is limestone from Caen in Normandy and in recent times the repairs have been carried out in Clipsham stone from Rutland.

It is characteristic of the less transcendental outlook of the Late Gothic Age that the spire was no longer *de rigueur*; for parish churches indeed it was now the exception. Among the cathedrals there are two besides Salisbury and Lichfield which owe much to their spires. At Norwich, as already mentioned, the original wooden spire came crashing down in a gale in 1362; more than a century *Ill. 171* elapsed before it was replaced. Then they built the second highest spire in England, rising to 315 ft. It is a relatively simple but very graceful design, richly crocketed in the fashion of the period. At *Ill. 170* Chichester the spire was of stone and earlier, having been completed about 1400; but in 1861 it was also destined to fall. Many years ago an old man related to me how, as a boy, he was looking out of the window of a train approaching Chichester when suddenly, before his eyes, the incredible happened: the spire telescoped into itself. (The cathedral authorities had in fact been warned that this would occur, and no one was injured.) The rebuilding (1861–1866) was very well done. Scott was the architect, and for once he did not try to improve on the original. The spired pinnacles at the base are in more intimate relationship with the spire itself than at Norwich, and the richly ornamented gables that project from the intervening faces are a pleasure. The small embattled turrets at the corners of the tower – also rebuilt by Scott – are the only weakness; a second and lower tier of pinnacles in their place would, one feels, have been preferable.

169 CANTERBURY: The central tower ('Bell Harry') from the south-west

171 NORWICH: View from the south-east

170 CHICHESTER: View from the south-west

172 NORWICH:
Transept vault, from the crossing

173 NORWICH: Part of the nave vault

The special triumphs of the Perpendicular architects were mainly centred on two features: towers and vaults. In some of their vault designs they combined almost unbelievable virtuosity with effects of marvellous beauty (and the two do not by any means necessarily correspond). The patterns made by lierne ribs could be varied almost at will, so this type of vault continued until the very end of the *Ills. 172, 173* Gothic period. Some of the loveliest are at Norwich, which had no high vaults until 1463: in the following half century or so the whole cathedral was vaulted. First came the nave, then the choir and presbytery, and finally the transepts. These vaults are an immense *Ill. 111* asset. If they are compared with Exeter it will be evident that basically they, too, are tierceron-vaults, on to which the lierne ribs have been applied with a purely ornamental intention. In the lofty presbytery the result is perfect. In the nave and transepts the Norman clerestories still survive, but the height of the vaults is so nicely judged, the curvature so sympathetic, that the effect is completely harmonious. The liernes on either side of the ridge-rib move in and out to form a series of elongated star patterns, alternating with diamond-shaped lozenges. Bosses have been scattered with marvellous profusion; in the (architectural) nave alone there are over three hundred, which in recent times have been effectively recoloured.

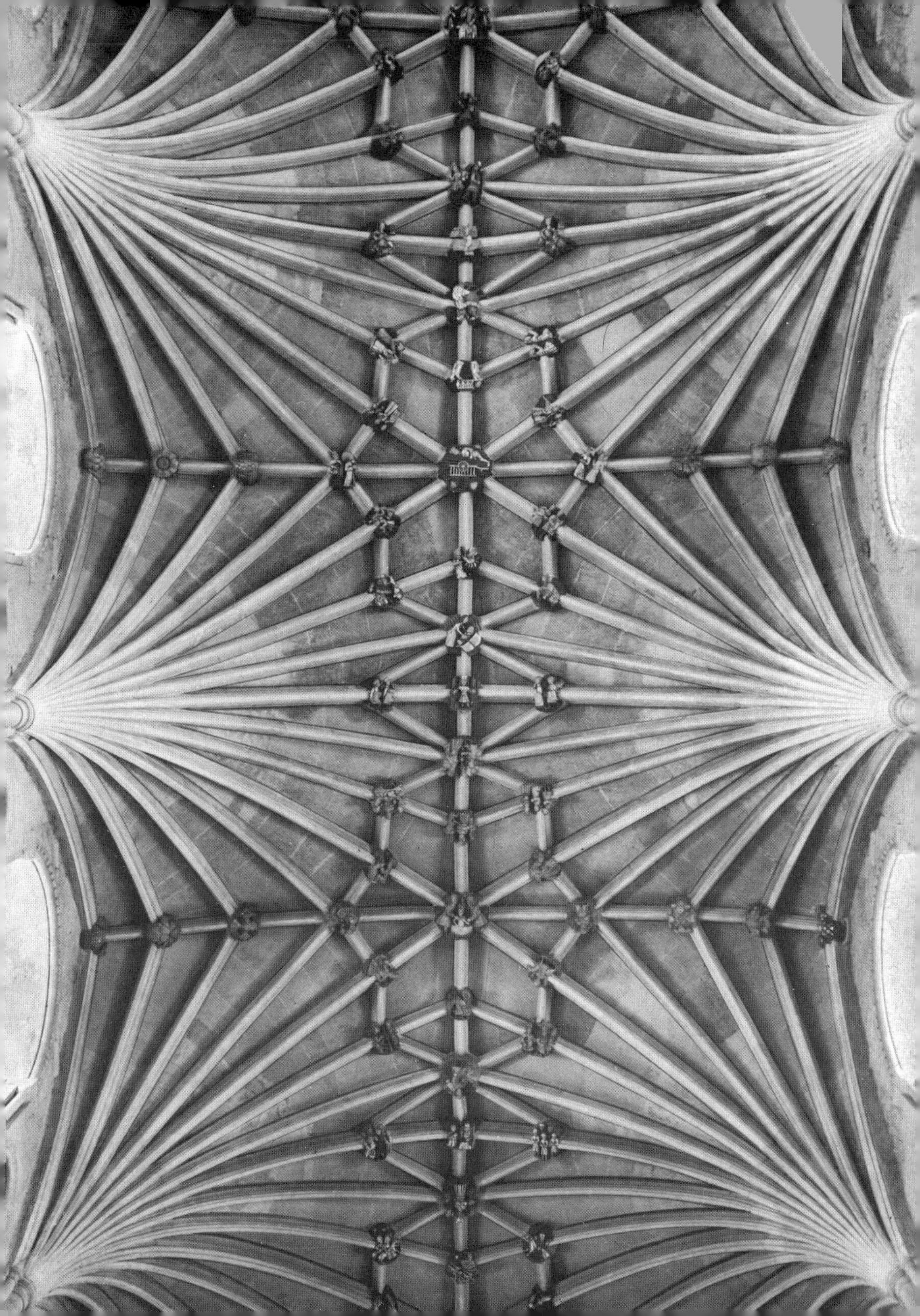

On a smaller scale, lierne-vaults can be seen to excellent effect in
Ill. 174 several cloisters, of which Norwich is again among the most striking. Here there are nearly four hundred more bosses; some of these have to fall back on the interest of their subject-matter to provide compensation for absence of artistic merit. At Wells, too, the cloisters –
Ill. 175 very spacious because, as mentioned earlier, the north walk was omitted – were rebuilt in the fifteenth century. The stonework is now somewhat blackened from long exposure, but the vaulting is most attractive. In each bay the liernes are arranged in the form of an octagon with a square centre. As usual a boss covers every point of intersection.

Well before the end of the fourteenth century, however, a still more original, ingenious and, many would add, beautiful type of vault had been evolved by English masons: the fan-vault. The earliest example known is a small one in the chantry chapel of Edward Lord Despenser at Tewkesbury; he died in 1375. Probably the same mason was responsible for the much more important fan-
Ill. 176 vaulting in the lovely cloisters at Gloucester, finished not later than 1412. The essential feature of the fan-vault is the inverted half-cone – or, more correctly, half-conoid: that is to say, a cone with concave sides. Each pair of half-conoids just touch at the centres of their curves. It was a logical development from the tierceron-vault; yet, romantic as it may appear, the fan-vault actually represented a step in the direction of standardization, for in this type of vault all the ribs are equidistant from each other, and in most cases all have the same curvature. The ribs are not applied separately: they were part and parcel of the solid block and, as the photograph shows, many of the joints between the blocks pass right across the purely decorative tracery. Such a method demanded large blocks of stone, and it is not unlikely that one of the reasons why the Gloucester masons were able to be so progressive and so inventive at this time was that the admirable Cotswold oolite could be quarried in the required sizes. The problem posed by the fan-vault is what to do about the spandrel. If the half-fans are to be given their full semicircular form, each bay must be square, which means that, relatively to the whole, the spandrels between the fans must be large. At Gloucester it was

174 NORWICH: The cloisters

possible to cope with these flat spandrels because the vault-span is only 12 ft, but in larger spans this was to present serious difficulties.
Ill. 176 A particularly fine feature here is the monks' *lavatorium*, with its own fan-vault echoing in miniature the adjacent one in the north walk. Although one may regret that these cloisters are glazed, in order to preserve the stonework it is necessary that they should be; and in fact the glazing does little to mar the subtle beauty of the lighting.

176 GLOUCESTER: The cloisters and monks' *lavatorium*

175 WELLS: The cloisters

The fan-vaults at Gloucester must surely have been accounted a brilliant success, yet several decades were to elapse before the experiment was repeated on a more ambitious scale. The first really big vault of this type was constructed in the 1440s over the presbytery of Sherborne Abbey in Dorset. The most famous large-scale fan-vault, without pendants, is that of King's College Chapel at Cambridge, erected by John Wastell between 1508 and 1515. In the few years before 1508 the same architect was responsible for two

177 PETERBOROUGH: The retro-choir, looking south

178 CANTERBURY: Central tower vault

memorable cathedral fan-vaults. The retro-choir at Peterborough is, it is true, undocumented, but on stylistic grounds there can be no reasonable doubt that it was the work of Wastell. One cannot fail to notice, nor regret, that the fans here, as also at King's College, are sliced away at the sides. Since the span is not much under 30 ft, this was a structural necessity. Had each fan been carried round the full 180 degrees, the flat spandrels between them would have become too large for safety. As it is, the bays are no longer square, as in the cloisters at Gloucester, but rectangular. Yet this is still a glorious vault, technically brilliant, and the obvious precursor of the much larger one at Cambridge. Another attractive feature of this retro-choir which was also repeated at King's is the decorative panelling below the windows, with elaborate double cusping. *Ill. 177*

At Canterbury, as we have seen, the great central tower was finished externally towards the end of 1497, but some work still remained to be done inside, and it was not until six or seven years later that Wastell constructed the fan-vault here, his smallest but also his loveliest. Bell Harry, like the great central towers of Lincoln and York, is of the lantern type, which means that as usual the lighting is enchanting. Admittedly the fans are again truncated, but here this does not matter because the four central ones melt into the four corner ones in a design of exquisite intricacy, rendered all the more telling some years ago by the application of colour to the stonework, probably in accord with the original practice. To gaze up at this vault at Canterbury is like peering into some finely wrought Gothic casket. *Ill. 178*

Most astonishing of all are the pendant-vaults. Of these the earliest, with a broad but low span, had been built by William Orchard for the Divinity School at Oxford between 1479 and 1483, and the most elaborate was to be that of Henry VII's Chapel at Westminster (1503–*c.*1512) by William Vertue. Between them

Ill. 179 came the pendant lierne-vault over the choir at Oxford, the only cathedral example. At this time it was still the priory church of St Frideswide; soon, with its nave shorn of four bays by Wolsey, it was to become a college chapel. But in the closing years of the fifteenth century the choir of this predominantly Late Norman and hitherto timber-roofed church was given one of the most remarkable vaults in the country. The designer, as at the Divinity School, was almost certainly William Orchard, one of the leaders of an outstanding group of contemporary architects, probably the most brilliant that England has ever had. As the photograph shows, each bay is occupied by an elaborate star pattern of exceptionally lovely form, worked out with boldly projecting lierne ribs, between which there are effective hollows of shadow. But the new feature is the series of pendants: lanterns of stone suspended for several feet with a daring which seems almost incredible, in that girderless age. How *do* they stay up? The clue is provided by the sections of strong moulded ribs which break through at the sides. Behind the lierne vaulting each pair of these continues, to make an arch; every pair of pendants represents the elongation of two of the voussoirs (wedge-shaped stones) of that arch, held in position by the pressure of the others. At the bases of the arch the thrust is of course counteracted by buttresses. Structurally, this is a feat of extraordinary architectural ingenuity, to which no Late Gothic buildings on the continent of Europe offer any close parallel. But it is much more than this: not only is it a *tour de force* of masoncraft but a superb work of art. It serves to show that almost until the end the Gothic flame continued to burn as brightly as ever.

179 OXFORD: The choir, looking east

CHAPTER NINE

The Protestant Reaction

ALL THE CATHEDRALS discussed so far were built for Roman Catholic worship, for in Western Europe until the sixteenth century there was no alternative. With the Reformation came a change of attitude towards these buildings. What in fact was the cathedral situation in England during the three hundred years from 1540 to 1840?

Whether we view them from the religious or from the aesthetic standpoint, there is ample evidence to show that although they had an occasional champion the majority of people regarded them at best with indifference, and often, as indicated in the opening chapter, with patronizing condescension. Iconoclasm, involving deliberate destruction, appeared in three successive waves: under Thomas Cromwell, when the principal target was the monasteries; under Elizabeth I, in an attempt to purge the country once for all of her sister's 'popery'; and under Thomas Cromwell's collateral descendant Oliver. All three onslaughts were primarily directed against images and relics, but during the first wave, from motives of greed, buildings were also a major target for destruction. And, as Martin Briggs points out,[11] enlightened Renaissance intellectuals like Erasmus and Colet could not but view the removal of superstitious images with a certain approval, even when they were works of artistic merit.

The cathedrals probably suffered less from iconoclasm than from sheer neglect, aggravated in some cases by the events of the Civil War, when they were liable to be used by *both* sides as barracks, stables and, worst of all, for confining prisoners of war. Among those that suffered substantial damage during the Civil War were: Old St Paul's in London, Canterbury, Chichester, Winchester, Exeter, Hereford, Worcester, Chester, Oxford, Norwich, Peterborough, Lincoln, Durham, and above all Lichfield and Carlisle. But in the Georgian period the principal reason for the widespread decay

180 LONDON. ST PAUL'S: Interior, looking east

which occurred was indifference, from which the clergy were by no means exempt. Such stained glass as had escaped the fanaticism of the iconoclasts was less often removed wholesale, as happened at Salisbury in 1788, than slowly allowed to perish through lack of care; and panels of cathedral glass would sometimes find their way into neighbouring country-houses by methods which Georgian clergymen do not seem to have regarded as reprehensible. Screens, pulpits and reredoses were removed for no better reason than that these men liked a vista. About 1790 the interior of Canterbury was covered with whitewash: 'it is so coarsely daubed,' wrote Horace Walpole in 1794, '... that I was shocked at the nudity of the whole'. Briggs quotes a letter written by Pugin in 1834 after a visit to Ely:

> Here is a church, magnificent in every respect, falling into decay through gross neglect. There is no person appointed to attend to the repair of the building, and the only person who has been employed during the last sixty years is a bricklayer. Not even common precautions are taken to keep the building dry. . . . In my travels I am daily witnessing fresh instances of the disgraceful conduct of the greater part of the established clergy. . . .

What was true of Ely at this time applied no less to a number of other cathedrals. No wonder that so much of what is to be seen today is Victorian restoration. Unfortunately this work was often undertaken in an opinionated and insensitive way, but it is only fair to recognize that if the Victorians had not taken the cathedrals in hand and spent a great deal of money on them, many would now be unusable if not actually in ruins.

It will readily be seen, then, that throughout these three centuries considerably more of our cathedral heritage was destroyed than created. Only one new cathedral arose during this period: St Paul's, London, the great exception in an otherwise unhappy story.

The motives of men's actions are complex; upon close examination, worthy and rather less worthy impulses will usually be found to operate in conjunction. Even in the pious Middle Ages, the cathedrals were not all erected to the glory of God in quite so single-minded a fashion as we have sometimes been led to believe. More worldly factors also played a part: rivalry with a neighbour, self-esteem of a rich benefactor, insurance against what might befall in the next world. With St Paul's, because of the temper of the time, these non-religious considerations loomed large: civic pomp, the pride of the City of London, the Establishment's desire to have a great church for solemn occasions. What could be more characteristic than that the first of these occasions, heralded by salutes from the Tower's guns, should have been a series of thanksgiving services, attended by the Queen, in honour of England's victories in various battles? For such purposes the architect, Christopher Wren, was in no doubt that an essential feature must be a large central space under an imposing dome.

By the middle of the seventeenth century the old cathedral, which was considerably larger than the present one, was already in a very bad state of decay, and the central tower was believed to be in imminent danger of collapse. Four months before the Great Fire Wren produced his first scheme, accompanied by a long and really alarming report. Of his various recommendations the most important related to the tower and the nave. 'It must be concluded', he wrote, 'that the Tower from Top to Bottom and the adjacent parts are such a heap of deformities that no Judicious Architect will think it corrigible by any Expense that can be laid out upon new dressing it.'

He therefore proposed replacing it with a dome. His uncle was Bishop of Ely and it is often said that it was his admiration for the Ely octagon which first gave him the idea for a central dome at St Paul's. With characteristic ingenuity, Wren suggested building the dome before taking down the tower. This, he said, would have a double advantage: it would be economical, as it would thereby be feasible to dispense with a lot of scaffolding, and it would mean that the people of London would never be deprived of their lofty, sentimentally prized landmark. As for the old Norman nave, he suggested recasing the weak rubble-filled piers with new stone, while at the same time giving it a Classical face-lift of the kind that Inigo Jones had already accorded the west front before the Rebellion.

The old cathedral was not totally destroyed by the Fire. In fact the west end, the least damaged part, was patched up sufficiently for temporary use within a few months. But it was a 'dangerous structure', and finally, in November 1673, the decision was taken to build entirely anew. The story of the rebuilding of St Paul's, and the many and often painful experiences to which its long-suffering and in the end most ill-treated architect had to submit, is too long, and perhaps too well known, to be repeated here.

The cathedral as built is the supreme example of that flexibility, that adaptability to circumstance, which was one of Wren's most striking traits. St Paul's is at once a compromise and a synthesis; a synthesis not only of the Classical and the Baroque but – what is much more remarkable – of the Classical and the Gothic. For if the façade elevations derive from Rome, the type of plan certainly comes from the Middle Ages, and so do the clerestory windows above lower aisles and the method of vault construction. There would seem to be nothing mediaeval about the series of shallow saucer-domes perched above twisted pendentives which Wren used throughout the building; yet in fact the thrusts are concentrated at the corners of each bay just as in a Gothic building, necessitating flying buttresses but enabling the intervening wall construction to be very much lighter. In Classical architecture flying buttresses would look quite incongruous; they are therefore hidden behind lofty screen walls which also have a part to play as buttresses. Except from above, the flying buttresses of St Paul's are rightly invisible.

The plan is notable for its symmetry. From the west one passes into a large vestibule, with flanking chapels to left and right, a device by which Wren was able to reduce the apparent length of the nave; the long nave had been imposed upon him at clerical insistence but he always disliked it. The rest of the building, apart from the narrow eastern bay and the apse, is entirely symmetrical: not only do the transepts balance one another but so also do the nave and choir. This concern with formal harmonies is of course typically Classical.

Wren never visited Rome, but in its general appearance the interior of St Paul's owes more to Roman architecture than to any other. The lofty round-headed arches, the large-scale coffering of

Ills. 180, 181

181 LONDON. ST PAUL'S: North aisle, looking west

183 LONDON. ST PAUL'S: Carving by Grinling Gibbons from the choir stalls

their soffits, the fluted pilasters with Corinthian capitals: all these are particularly characteristic of ancient Rome. Such features are stately, dignified, and excellent for pomp and ceremony, but like Roman architecture itself they do not warm the heart. The interior of St Paul's remains detached and aloof: it is easier to admire than to like. Its most impressive feature is the central space under the dome. For the greatest pleasure, study the woodcarving and the ironwork.

The closing years of the seventeenth century were a great age for craftsmanship, and not only St Paul's but all Wren's major buildings, as he would have been the first to acknowledge, owe much to the craftsmen whom he directed. The choir of the cathedral was decorated in the most sumptuous style. The splendid stalls and the screen behind them, together with most of the organ-case, were designed by Wren and carved, with a wealth of original detail, by Grinling Gibbons, of whom Horace Walpole was to say that 'there was no instance before him of a man who gave to wood the loose and airy lightness of flowers, and chained together the various productions of the elements with the free disorder natural to each species'. Gibbons was the son of a London draper who had gone to live in Rotterdam, where he was born and brought up; Jean Tijou, the smith, was French, and for more than twenty years after 1689 worked almost continuously for Wren. He made the massive iron window-frames of St Paul's, a purely utilitarian task, but he was also responsible for the delicate balustrades and the gorgeous wrought-

Ill. 183

Ill. 182

182 LONDON. ST PAUL'S: Wrought-iron gates by Jean Tijou on the south side of the choir

184 LONDON. ST PAUL'S: Interior of dome

185 LONDON. ST PAUL'S: Exterior of dome

iron gates and screens, characterized as usual by a boldly architectural framework and by an abundance of small embossed pieces of solid metal, mainly leaves and scrolls, which, although they do not seem to have been gilded originally, lend themselves very well to it.

Both inside and out, the glory of St Paul's is the dome. It does not look Roman; yet here again, although Wren's principal debt was to the great architects of the Renaissance, Bramante, Michelangelo and J.-H. Mansart, the original inspiration did come from Rome. For it is the Pantheon that was the great forerunner of European dome construction, so utterly unlike the bubble-blown, ethereal domes of the Orient. The special feature of Wren's dome is its loftiness; St Paul's, as he willingly recognized, was expected to have a high central feature, and Wren, bent on having a dome and not a tower, seized the chance of erecting one which would not only dominate the cathedral but, for two hundred and fifty years, the entire City of London.

A coronal cluster of steeples tall
Like a chime over London sweetly call,
And high over all
Are the Cross and the Ball
On the Riding Redoubtable Dome of St Paul.

To achieve this loftiness called for the most brilliant ingenuity, and, as is well known, there are in fact two domes. The octagonal central space is 102 ft in diameter; it is roofed by a dome of which the apex would have been 214 ft above the floor. But the dome which London sees is some 60 ft higher than that; above the inner dome Wren built a tall cone of brick, from the outer surface of which another dome, lighly constructed of wood sheathed with Derbyshire lead, is held out on timber struts rather in the manner of a crinoline. The brick cone also serves to support the beautifully designed lantern, 364 ft high, which is only 40 ft less than Salisbury's spire.[12]

Ill. 184

Ill. 185

The lantern, the most original feature of Wren's design, shows him in a more Baroque vein. Not only is it delightful in itself, but it is artistically of great value in providing the stylistic link between the predominantly Classical dome and the decidedly Baroque west

Ill. 186 towers. That there should be a pair of façade towers at all at this date is significant; moreover, they stand outside the ends of the aisles, as at Wells. Their form was not finally determined until the very last moment, when much of the building was already up, and they were not finished until about 1710. They are among Wren's most fascinating inventions, and show how completely unacademic was his approach to architecture. A large drawing of the south-west tower in the Cathedral Library reveals that at the age of seventy-five he was still designing every detail himself, and with no obvious precedents – unless perhaps he derived a few hints from Borromini's towers of S. Agnese in Rome, to which they bear a slight resemblance. Convex and concave surfaces are most subtly blended with segments of circles. Urns are introduced with unfailing skill to assist and enrich the transitions. The change of shape as each stage is set back from the one below is very characteristic of Wren, and the pair of cupolas suggestive of bells is wonderfully effective.

One of the chief attractions of St Paul's is the fine quality of its stone, almost all of which came by sea from Portland in Dorset. The thorough cleaning that has been carried out in recent years has revealed a wealth of carving which the grime of centuries had rendered almost invisible. Wren's exterior has two storeys throughout, with a bold cornice separating them. Both have smooth ashlared

Ill. 187 pilasters, and at the extremities of the building only, columns, and intervening walling that is rusticated throughout. Otherwise the treatment of the two storeys varies considerably. But both are sumptuously adorned with ornamental carving which, after more than two and a half centuries, is still in a splendid state of preservation. Within clearly defined limits the character of the work varies, for the good reason that many different carvers were employed; the names of all the principal men are known. Six masonry-contractors were employed simultaneously on different parts of the building and each made his own labour arrangements. Grinling Gibbons was not

186 London. St Paul's: The south-west tower

only the presiding genius of the internal woodcarving but was responsible for some of the stonecarving too; the Stuart coat of arms between angels in the pediment over the north transept is his, and so are all but two of the 'Festoones' (as they are called in the accounts) under the lower windows. There are nearly thirty of these panels, and they make a wonderful set, richly decorative but meaningful too, for their themes include the patron saint, Paul, the monarchs and ecclesiastics whose actions furthered the building enterprise, and the Virtues with their appropriate attributes. *Ill. 188*

187 LONDON
ST PAUL'S:
The apse,
from the sout

188 LONDON. ST PAUL'S: 'Festoone' by Grinling Gibbons

Above the windows of the lower storey there is a large cherub's head on every keystone, and to either side swags and drops of fruit and flowers and fluttering ribbons. These are not by Gibbons, but some of the other carvers who worked on St Paul's seem hardly, if at all, inferior. In accord with the spirit of the age, they all appear to have enjoyed carving the heads of young children, whose soft, plump faces look out at us with lifelike naturalism from above their cherubic wings. John Thompson, who was entrusted with the adornment of the Dean's door on the south side of the south-west tower, is not one of the best known of these carvers, but his sculpture, so delicate, so refined, so delightfully accomplished, is surely the perfect foil for the bold, assured character of the architecture. *Ill. 189*

189 LONDON. ST PAUL'S: The Dean's Door, with carving by John Thompson

190 LIVERPOOL: The Roman Catholic cathedral. Exterior

CHAPTER TEN

The Last Hundred Years

IF THE Roman Catholic cathedrals are included, the story must be carried back rather more than a hundred years. Catholic emancipation in England dates from 1829 and cathedrals were erected in Birmingham and in Newcastle-upon-Tyne in 1839–1841 and 1844 respectively. For both buildings the architect was Pugin; in both cases economies were essential; and in truth neither affords much artistic pleasure. St George's Cathedral in Southwark, also by Pugin and dating again from 1841, was at first only a parish church. Here too shortage of money was originally a problem; but rebuilding after serious war damage has given it much more dignity than it ever had before, and some colourful stained glass.

Far and away the most ambitious of the Roman Catholic cathedrals is Westminster, built between 1895 and 1903 from the designs of J. F. Bentley. This is a neo-Byzantine building which seems in all essentials to belong to the Mediterranean, and to have nothing of England in its make-up. The style was chosen, we are told, because in addition to affording ample space for ceremonial, a brick cathedral in this style could be erected much more quickly and at far lower cost than a stone building in Gothic. Twelve and a half million bricks were used. Apart from the lofty Italian-looking campanile, 284 ft high to the top of the cross, the exterior, faced with red brick and white limestone in horizontal stripes, is big but lumpy. The interior is much more impressive, with four large domes along the main axis. The two nave domes are flanked by low aisles with large tribunes above, and chapels outside the aisles; the building is therefore exceptionally wide (156 ft compared with a total length of 360 ft). There are some very handsome marble columns of various colours, all brought from abroad, but otherwise, despite some individual splendours, the decoration is not at present satisfactory. Some parts are faced with marbles that vary greatly in colour and provenance, while much is still bare brown brick; the contrast between such sumptuousness and such bareness is uncomfortable. Yet if all were marble up to about 30 ft the effect might well be oppressive. For the walls above that height, the arches, vaults and domes, Bentley envisaged mosaics, but good mosaic artists are now rare and the medium has become very costly.

Ill. 190 The most recent Roman Catholic cathedral is Frederick Gibberd's at Liverpool (1962–1967), commissioned from two hundred and ninety-eight competition entries. This marks an entirely new departure in English cathedral architecture. The building, which is of steel and concrete, is circular, and rises conically to a sixteen-sided lantern tower with tapering walls, between the struts, consisting wholly of glass. Above this is a most effective corona of stainless steel, delightfully cobwebby below, and culminating, at a height of about 290 ft, in a ring of slender crossed finials. The whole structure is supported by sixteen long trusses of reinforced concrete which splay out radially from the base of the tower like huge oars. Happily the external concrete surfaces have all been faced, the chapels and porches with Portland stone, the ribs with pale grey stone mosaic. The roof is of neutral grey aluminium.

The moment of entering is thrilling. The main sensations are of space – the building is not only very lofty but nearly 200 ft in diameter – and of colour: one is in a great bath of coloured light, red, yellow, purple and green, but predominantly blue, some of which is reflected from the grey and white marble floor. This rich glass is all non-figurative, and much of it is entirely plain. The sanctuary is in the centre, directly below the tower. The chapels around the perimeter vary in size, shape and function – not a happy feature externally, but one which adds interest within. Seating more than 3,000 people, this is a remarkable and boldly conceived building, far less costly than Liverpool's Anglican cathedral and less solemn, less authoritative, yet in my opinion decidedly the more enjoyable.

The Church of England has seen the creation of many new sees since Ripon was raised to cathedral status in 1836. Most of them are

191 TRURO: View from the north-east

centred on large industrial towns that had no church with either the dimensions or the appearance of a real cathedral. This gave rise to what are known as the parish-church cathedrals, to many of which big additions have been or are now being made, with varying success.

The last hundred years have, however, also seen the erection of four entirely new English cathedrals. First came Truro, designed in 1880 by J.L. Pearson and finished in 1910 by his son. This is a scholarly building, on a cramped and unworthy site, but unfortunately there is little about it which is creative. Essentially it is an academic exercise in the Early English style, with three attractive spires that have a Norman French look. The incorporation of one Tudor aisle of the former parish church (the rest was pulled down) only serves to demonstrate how alien this cathedral is to Cornwall. St Mary's aisle, with its whitened walls and its typically Cornish wagon roof, has nothing to do with the cathedral either in style or spirit. *Ill. 191*

Liverpool's Anglican cathedral was begun in 1904 and is now about nine-tenths finished, but so vast is the scale of this undertaking

that it is not likely to be completed before the mid-seventies at the earliest. It will then be the largest cathedral in the world after St Peter's, Rome. The architect, Giles Gilbert Scott, was only twenty-two when his design was selected out of more than a hundred submitted in competition. Between then and his death in 1960 the original designs were several times modified and certainly greatly improved, as progress continued. The building occupies a fine site on a high rocky ridge overlooking the Mersey; on the side away
Ill. 193 from the river an abandoned graveyard in an old quarry, deep and wooded, adds an extra touch of drama. The ridge runs north–south, so that the liturgical east end in fact faces south. It seems certain that this will be the last cathedral in Britain to be constructed entirely of stone. The material is the local Woolton sandstone, very pink but also somewhat sombre, which no doubt accounts for the deliberately light pointing. So far it has stood up well to the city's salty, sooty atmosphere. The roofs, now green, are of copper.

The plan is markedly original; the cathedral which this Gothic building most closely resembles in its planning is, surprisingly enough, Wren's St Paul's. Apart from some projecting buildings at the (liturgical) east end, which include a large Lady Chapel – the first portion to reach completion, and the most elaborately wrought – and a small octagonal chapter-house, there is, as at St Paul's,
Ill. 192 absolute symmetry, with a huge central space and a nave and choir of equal length (three main bays each, in both cathedrals). The great difference is that at Liverpool the central space is flanked on both sides by transepts, between whose projecting arms are placed the principal porches. Internally this yields an unimpeded area 201 ft long and 87 ft wide, capable of seating a vast congregation. The vaults are 116 ft high and under the central tower the lovely 'umbrella' vault soars to 175 ft.

The immediate impression upon entering is of great dignity allied to a certain staidness. The aisles, low tunnels seemingly burrowed into the masonry, afford no pleasure. The architect has taken traditional Gothic forms and reinterpreted them in a new and unfamiliar way, and there are originalities in the handling of some of the details too; yet it has to be admitted that in many of the

192 LIVERPOOL: The Anglican cathedral. Interior looking east

furnishings neither inspiration nor sensibility seem to be much in evidence. This particularly applies to the sculpture and the pre-1939 stained glass, some of which was removed by enemy bombs.

The exterior could be described as ponderous, but the scale is so enormous that this is hardly a criticism. The building is well proportioned and the great cliffs of masonry are massed with much skill. *Ill. 193* The best feature of all, the central tower, was only substituted for the twin towers of the original design after the building had been in progress for some years. The upper stage is eight-sided, with octagonal turrets set against the four shorter faces. This huge tower, from the level of the cathedral floor to the top of the pinnacles 331 ft high, is among the most majestic in England, and unlike any other.

The other two new cathedrals, Guildford and Coventry, are much smaller than Liverpool and cost a great deal less to build. The archi-

193 LIVERPOOL: The Anglican cathedral from the south-east

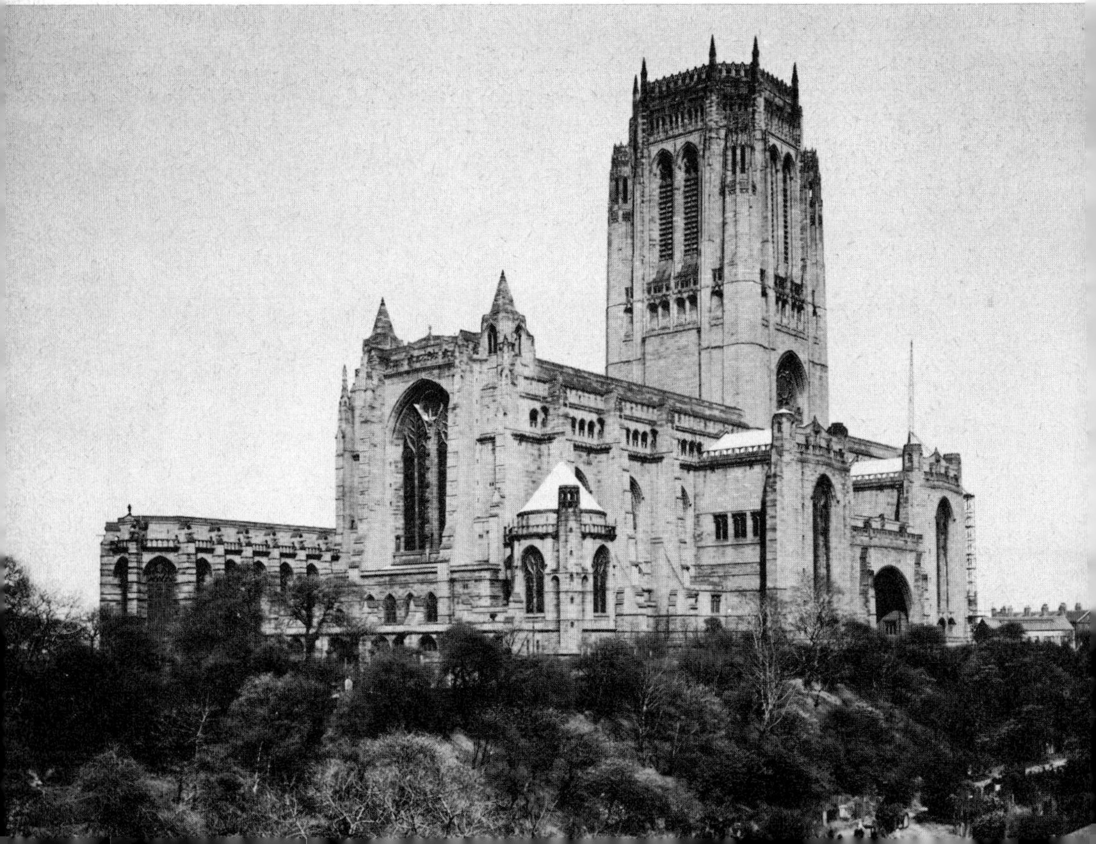

194 GUILDFORD: Interior, looking east

tects of both, like those of the two at Liverpool, were chosen by open competition, a method never used for English cathedrals in the past but certainly the best in the circumstances now prevailing. For Guildford the competition was held in 1932; one hundred and eighty-three architects entered, and the winner was Edward Maufe. Building began, on another fine hill-top site, in 1936, but was soon to suffer long interruption as a result of the Second World War. Most of the work was carried out between 1952 and 1965.

Maufe's design, in a simplified version of Gothic, is mild and unadventurous, but takes account, as Pearson at Truro did not, of the *genius loci*. The shapes are largely dictated, as they should be, by the material, which is a red brick of good quality made from the clay of the hill itself. The austere exterior is therefore distinguished by crisp outlines, good massing and a minimum of ornamentation. The *Ill. 195*

195 GUILDFORD: Exterior, from the west

Ill. 194 interior comes as a surprise, for here the brickwork is hidden under plaster rendering, with Doulting limestone introduced for the dressings. But clean lines still predominate, combined now with a cool spaciousness which is very satisfying. Unfortunately few of the furnishings, and as yet none of the windows, are worthy of the architecture.

No greater contrast could be imagined than between Guildford and Coventry. Although by no means in the vanguard of modernism, here at last is an Anglican cathedral designed in a contemporary idiom. It is certainly one of the best known English buildings of the twentieth century. Its predecessor was one of the parish-church cathedrals: a very large Perpendicular church which was not accorded cathedral status until 1918. In November 1940 German bombs reduced this building to a blackened shell, apart fortunately from the noble tower and spire, one of the finest in England. At first the intention was to build anew in traditional English Gothic. Only after long controversy was the design thrown open, in 1951, to competition. The winner was Basil Spence, and his cathedral, with all the furnishings contributed by other artists, arose in no more than six years: 1956 to 1962.

Coventry is important because it represents a rethinking of the whole 'cathedral idea' in terms of mid-twentieth-century requirements, materials, techniques, and let it be added, economics. Some notable concessions were made to the traditions of the past, above all the admirable decision to face the whole building with stone. Two nicely contrasted varieties were used: pink sandstone from Hollington in Staffordshire, which looks very much at home in Coventry where the New Red sandstone is the local material, and green slate from Little Langdale in Westmorland which is a 'foreigner' but a welcome one. Originally it was intended to use pink stone for internal facing too, but later it was felt that a grey-white roughcast, besides being much cheaper, would set off to better advantage the stained-glass windows.

196 COVENTRY: Entrance side from the south-west, with the old cathedral ruins in the foreground

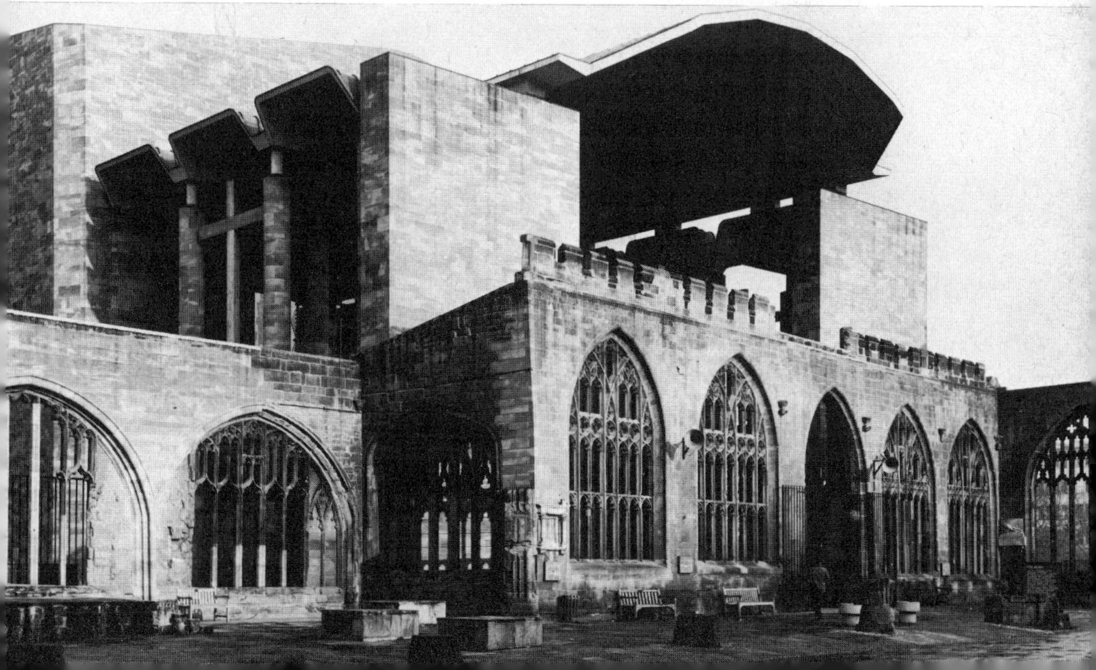

The new cathedral is set at right angles to the old, the surviving shell of which serves as a forecourt. From here a staircase descends into the lofty porch, which, the architect says, was suggested to him by the mainly unbuilt nave of the Cathedral of Siena, that vast undertaking of the fourteenth century which, had it ever been completed, would have converted the present cathedral, to which it too runs at right angles, into a transept. The Coventry porch is also accessible from east and west; just outside the eastern entrance is Epstein's St Michael and Lucifer, a late work in bronze. From across the road there is a good view of the immense swelling window of the baptistery and, beyond, five of the ten windows, each 70 ft high, which are arranged on a saw-tooth pattern in order that the coloured light from each should be directed towards the altar. This is one of the most original and best-known features of the design. *Ill. 196* *Ill. 197*

The building is entered from the vestibule through a wide and lofty glass screen engraved with saints and angels. It is at once revealed as a hall-church, traditional in that it is divided into nave and aisles but wholly contemporary in its proportions, made possible by the strength of reinforced concrete. The high piers, which taper downwards, are very slender and could be even more so, as is demonstrated at their base. The vault comprises a thin but very strong web of reinforced concrete, with timber slats for the infilling; the cells suggest a series of prisms. *Ill. 198* *Ill. 199*

The lighting is not entirely successful; there is too much daylight at the entrance end, while too little reaches the high altar and the tapestry above it. But internally the general effect of the architecture is at once dignified and elegant, and it is apparent that every detail has been carefully and lovingly considered. Opinions may differ on the relative artistic values of the contributions of Spence's team of artists: Graham Sutherland's huge tapestry, the stained glass by John Piper, Lawrence Lee, Geoffrey Clarke, Keith New and others, the engraved glass by John Hutton, and so on. What is certain is that they are works far richer in creative qualities than those which furnish any of the other cathedrals discussed in this chapter. It is not too much to say that Basil Spence approached his task in a spirit of dedication, which he seems to have been able to communicate to

197 COVENTRY: Exterior from the south-east, showing Epstein's 'St Michael and Lucifer'

198 COVENTRY: The vestibule and glass screen

every member of his team. The widespread popular interest in Coventry Cathedral, a building which literally millions have queued to see, must owe a great deal to this corporate effort on the part of so many gifted artists.

Yet, one asks oneself again and again, what is the nature of this popular interest – not only in Coventry but in other cathedrals such as Canterbury and St Paul's, into which in summer-time the crowds pour in their thousands week after week? Is it an interest in religion that draws most of them? I do not think so. Except on Sundays and on special occasions cathedral services are usually poorly attended, and it seems no exaggeration to assert that, for every one visitor who

199 COVENTRY: Interior, looking towards the altar

goes to worship, there are a hundred who go just to look. And why not? Any number of people, not necessarily religious, find in visits to cathedrals a source of deep spiritual refreshment; and no wonder, for they are in contact with some of the greatest works of artistic genius that England has ever produced. Many of these unfortunately miss much that the cathedrals have to offer because they do not know what they are looking at nor what to look for. That is something which the schools and universities could help to remedy if they chose; a few are already doing so, and one greatly hopes that more will soon be following suit.

In Wren's time Englishmen had already moved a long way from

the ethos in which the cathedrals of the Middle Ages arose. In some respects, moreover, this was all to the good, for the mediaeval churches were the products of fears and superstitions as well as of finer and nobler impulses. To me the remarkable fact is not that Coventry Cathedral, for all its merits, is a building with neither the strength nor the beauty nor the emotive power of a Durham, a Lincoln or a Canterbury, but that it ever arose at all, in this age of widespread unbelief. The martyrdom of Coventry no doubt had much to do with it; it would, I suspect, have been difficult to generate a like enthusiasm anywhere else. Yet the fact remains that the cathedral was built, and that countless thousands go to look, and some to worship. Experience is thereby broadened and lives enriched. This may owe little to the Church; but then, it may be felt, can the Church in fairness be expected to go on carrying the financial burden of maintaining these expensive fabrics for so many non-churchmen to enjoy? It could be said, no doubt, that in practice the Church does not shoulder this responsibility unaided, since the English people hold their cathedrals in such high regard that special appeals, sometimes for very large sums, almost invariably succeed. Nevertheless, the present situation cannot be regarded as satisfactory. Under the Historic Buildings and Ancient Monuments Act of 1953 any building of 'outstanding historic or architectural interest', whether secular or ecclesiastical, qualifies for grants towards the cost of repairs subject to certain controls. At present the annual sum made available is quite insufficient to meet the needs of the cathedrals, which accordingly not only receive no Government aid but are exempt from the controls to which, in the view of many responsible people, they ought to be liable. I hope and believe that within a generation we shall see England following the example of a number of other European countries in making the State, which means the taxpayers, responsible for maintaining these great creations of England's past. In comparison with what they have to give, it will be a small price to pay.

Notes

1 T. S. R. Boase: *English Art, 1100–1216* (*Oxford History of English Art*, vol. III), 1953, p. 89.

2 St Gabriel's Chapel at Canterbury, because it also contains precious early wall paintings, is usually kept locked, but it is possible to gain access on applying to a verger.

3 The Gervase quotations are from the translation by Charles Cotton, undertaken for the Friends of Canterbury Cathedral (Cambridge University Press, 1930 *et seq.*).

4 The 'scaffolding' of small shafts which covers the west front of Wells is frequently described as being of Purbeck marble, but this is not so. The original colonnettes were of a local lias. These decayed, and in 1870 most of them were replaced by black Irish marble from Kilkenny.

5 Alwalton is on the Nene near Peterborough. Like the much more familiar Purbeck this limestone also abounds in fossils, but of oysters instead of freshwater snails. With polishing these shells yield very pleasing patterns.

6 Peter Brieger: *English Art, 1216–1307* (*Oxford History of English Art*, vol. IV), 1957, p. 30.

7 Since at Salisbury the dedication of the cathedral is to the Virgin Mary, there was no need for a separate Lady Chapel, and accordingly the eastern chapel here is sometimes, and more correctly perhaps, called the Trinity Chapel. The use of the term Lady Chapel has however been retained in this book, as it is the one in general use for describing the eastern chapel, at Salisbury as elsewhere.

8 Joan Evans: *English Art, 1307–1461* (*Oxford History of English Art*, vol. V), 1949, p.22.

9 Nikolaus Pevsner: *The Buildings of England: North Somerset and Bristol*, 1958, pp. 371–2.

10 Most of what remains of Inigo Jones's Winchester rood screen, including the big central arch with fluted columns and an attic above, all finely carved, is now in the University Museum of Archaeology and Ethnology at Cambridge. Other portions are in the crypt of Winchester Cathedral, where for a few days every year they are partly immersed by floodwater. Good bronze statues of James I and Charles I from this screen, by Hubert Le Sueur, now stand against the west wall of the cathedral.

11 Martin S. Briggs: *Goths and Vandals*, 1952. A valuable book for those interested in the English cathedrals since the Reformation.

12 It is an odd fact that no two authorities seem exactly to agree about any of the dimensions of St Paul's.

Visiting the Cathedrals: Summaries and Plans

To arrive at a cathedral city for the first time can be an unforgettable experience; nothing can ever quite equal the thrill of the initial impact. Each church conveys its personality not only visually but also in its atmosphere. Largely through the accidents of geography, some cathedrals seem to bustle with visitors, while others are so unforthcoming that one treads gingerly into their emptiness. Many are seen at their best, especially internally, on sunny summer afternoons, perhaps with the west doors thrown wide open. But crisp winter mornings can be hardly less enjoyable. As with all architecture, sunshine is essential for a full appreciation, both within and without.

Leaving aside the parish-church cathedrals, the four modern Anglican buildings discussed in the last chapter and all those erected since the eighteen-thirties by the Roman Catholics, England has twenty-six cathedrals, of which, very conveniently, exactly half are of the first rank. These are: (1) three in the South-East and South: Canterbury, Winchester and Salisbury; (2) three in the West and South-West: Gloucester, Wells and Exeter; (3) three in or close to East Anglia: Norwich, Ely and Peterborough; (4) three in the North-East: Lincoln, York and Durham; (5) London. The other thirteen are also well worth a visit, but no cathedral-lover should miss any of those named above.

Throughout the summaries which follow, use has been made of the familiar abbreviations, E.E., Dec. and Perp.

Dates overlap, but the inclusive periods of the successive phases are these:

Norman	1066–1190
Early English	1175–1265
Decorated	1250–1370
Perpendicular	1330–1540

The plans accompanying the summaries have all been drawn to a uniform scale.

Bristol

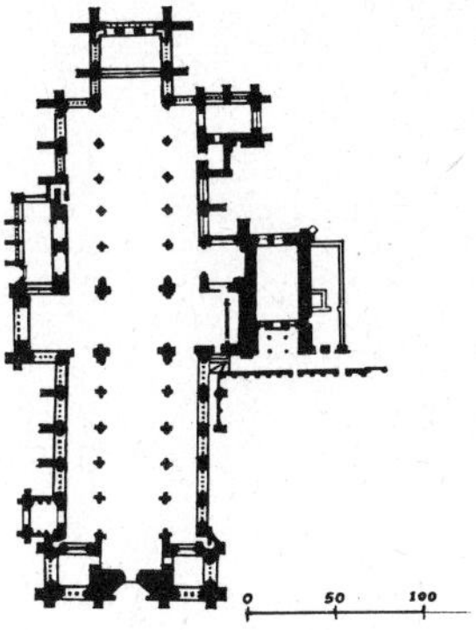

Only the eastern half of the cathedral is mediaeval: the nave is a Victorian rebuilding. Exterior well seen from College Green, but not very imposing. Interior, alone among the English cathedrals, has aisles of the same height as the central area, recalling a German hall-church. Dec. choir with a good lierne vault and, over the aisles, vaulting of unique and fascinating design. Chapter-house, late-Norman, has lost its E. bay but is still a spacious rectangular building notable internally for its rich non-figurative ornamentation.

Canterbury

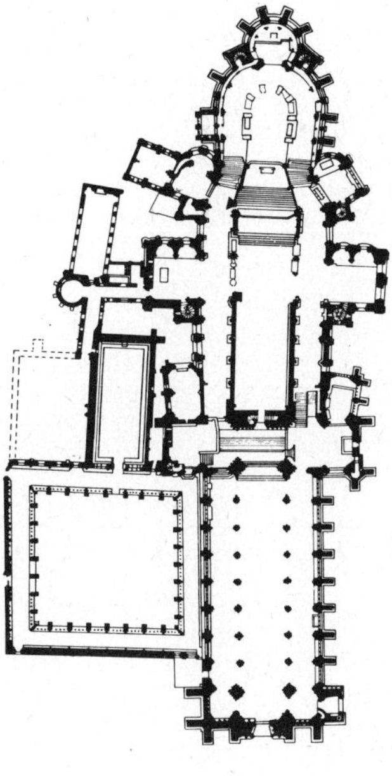

A very large cathedral which suffers from a lack of architectural unity, but the separate parts include several of consummate beauty and importance. The Norman crypt is England's best, with some sculptured capitals of outstanding quality. Lifted high above it are the choir and Trinity Chapel (retro-choir), which illustrate the beginnings of Gothic in England. Their late-12 c. and early-13 c. stained glass is by far the loveliest in the country. In the S.E. transept, four fine modern windows by Erwin Bossanyi. 12 c. wall paintings in St Gabriel's and St Anselm's chapels. Behind the high altar, a handsome floor of coloured stones set in geometrical patterns (*Opus Alexandrinum*). Many interesting monuments, notably those of the Black Prince (d. 1376) and Henry IV (d. 1413). The nave is a masterpiece of early Perp. The central tower is the finest in the land, and its lantern has an exquisite fan vault. The Perp. cloisters have an unrivalled collection of heraldic bosses, skilfully repainted. Very large rectangular chapter-house, Dec. and Perp. Interesting and extensive precincts, including, especially, the monks' water tower, octagonal, standing above an open, vaulted undercroft.

Carlisle

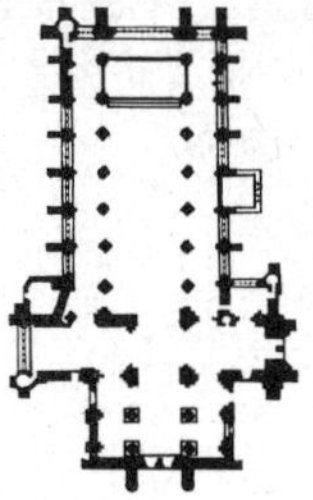

England's second smallest cathedral, since of the seven bays of the Norman nave only two survive. The choir, rebuilt on a different axis early in the 13 c. and again after a fire in 1292, is now much the most impressive part of the building, within and without. Richly moulded Dec. windows, especially the nine-light E. window, the cathedral's particular pride; but not much mediaeval glass. Forty-six well-preserved early-15 c. stalls, with large and lively misericords. Wagon-roof attractively painted. Poor central tower, too small and too squat.

Chester

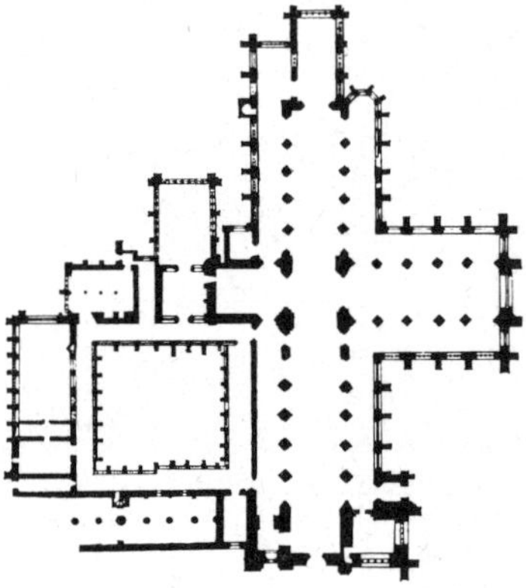

A building which has suffered greatly from Victorian restoration, partly rendered necessary by the softness of the pink sandstone. Somewhat amorphous plan. Exterior not enjoyable. Interior better, but much darkened by indifferent Victorian glass. Except over Lady Chapel, vaults are only of wood imitating stone. Early-Dec. choir has one superb feature, the stalls, *c.*1380, with exquisite figure-carving and 48 misericords which for delicacy and grace surpass even those at Lincoln and Beverley: a wonderful set. On N. side of cathedral, cloisters, refectory and elegant rectangular E.E. chapter-house, with shafted lancet windows and a charming entrance vestibule.

Chichester

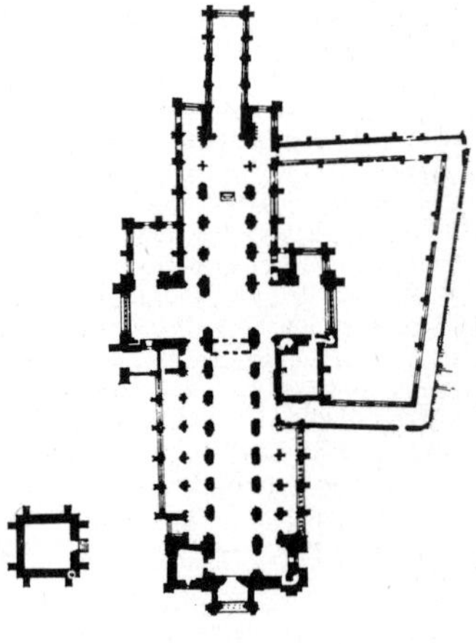

Compared with most of England's Norman cathedrals, Chichester was designed on a modest scale, despite its double aisles, formed in the 13 c. out of a range of chapels. The finest part is the retro-choir, erected after a fire in 1186 in the Transitional style between the Norman and the earliest Gothic. The three E. bays of the long narrow Lady Chapel are an attractive example of Dec. The greatest treasure is a pair of large Romanesque relief sculptures, of rare intensity of feeling, in the S. choir aisle. Pulpitum Perp.: removed in 1859 and reinstated 1961. Much bad glass: that in the big S. transept window, of 1877, is a prize specimen. Central tower and spire a Victorian rebuilding, very well done. To N. of W. front, detached bell-tower, 15 c.: unusual.

Durham

The noblest example in England of Norman cathedral-building, and indeed the grandest Romanesque church in Europe. Only the eastern transept, the three towers and the cloisters are later than the 12 c. Superbly sited; yet the exterior is not quite worthy of the interior. No W. front: instead, the unique Galilee Chapel, built as a Lady Chapel, with slender piers and much chevron decoration. Overwhelmingly impressive nave, with a great deal of non-figurative carved ornamentation. Original early-12 c. vaults over nave and transepts. Choir differs from nave in details but is no less grand. Handsome late-14 c. reredos (the Neville screen). At E. end, Chapel of the Nine Altars or eastern transept, a big 13 c. addition erected to house the shrine of St Cuthbert. Unusual choir stalls and font canopy: *temp*. Charles II. Cloisters, 15 c., to S., with former monks' dormitory above the west walk, now an important museum.

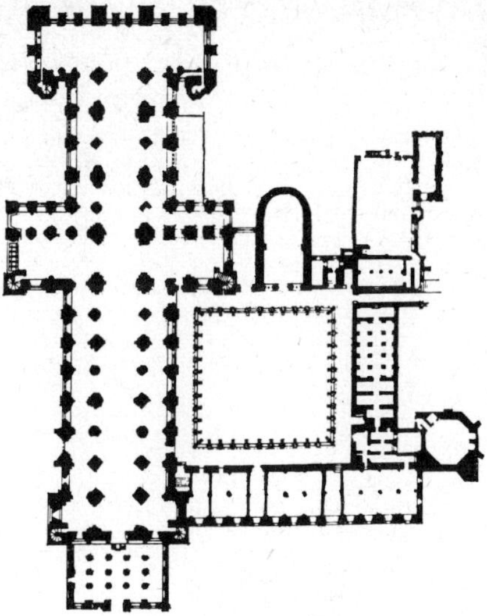

Ely

With its central Octagon and single tower at W. end, a building of marked individuality, dominating every prospect for miles around; for although scarcely 100 ft above sea-level, the surrounding countryside is among the flattest in England. When in mediaeval times this fenland was flooded, the cathedral would appear to be floating like a great ship at anchor, and even without the floodwaters no great imaginative effort is required, under the right conditions of light, to recapture this rivetting impression. Richly arcaded but unfortunately incomplete W. front, with S.W. transept. Interior one of the most majestic of the English cathedrals, solemn and austere in the Norman nave and transepts, exuberant E. of the crossing and in the big Lady Chapel. Most memorable of all is the interior of the Octagon, unique in Gothic architecture. Not many furnishings of interest, and a lot of very poor glass. Not much remains of the cloisters except the elaborately sculptured Norman doorways through which they were entered.

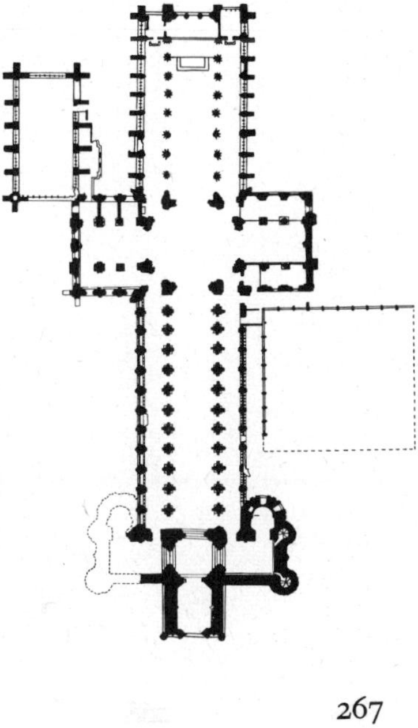

Exeter

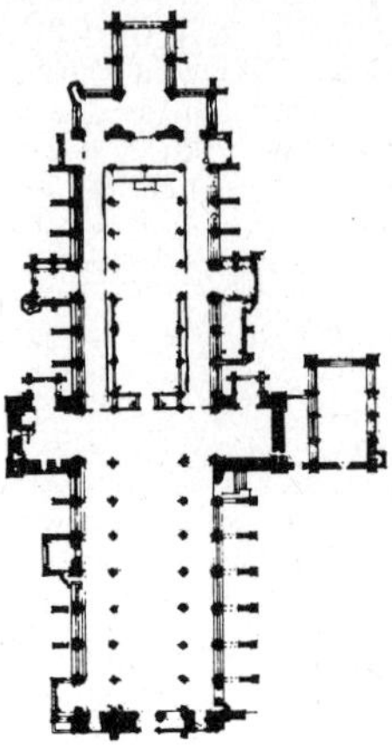

The towers, which, exceptionally, are placed over the transepts, are Norman; almost everything else that matters here is Dec.: 1275–1369. W. front is elaborate and unusual but not an architectural success; its statues mostly original, but badly worn by wind and rain. Exterior looks best from E. After the rather unimposing exterior the interior comes as a tremendous surprise, for this is one of the glories of England. The tierceron ribbed vault, 300 ft long, is among the most magnificent creations of Gothic architecture in any country. Richly moulded piers and arches; profusely carved corbels and bosses. Original pulpitum (1325) marred by obtrusive organ. Stone sedilia and oak Bishop's Throne masterpieces of Dec. carving. Choir stalls with the earliest misericords in England, a set of 49 dating from 1260–80. Part of glass in E. window is 14 c.; otherwise nearly all Exeter's glass is indifferent.

Gloucester

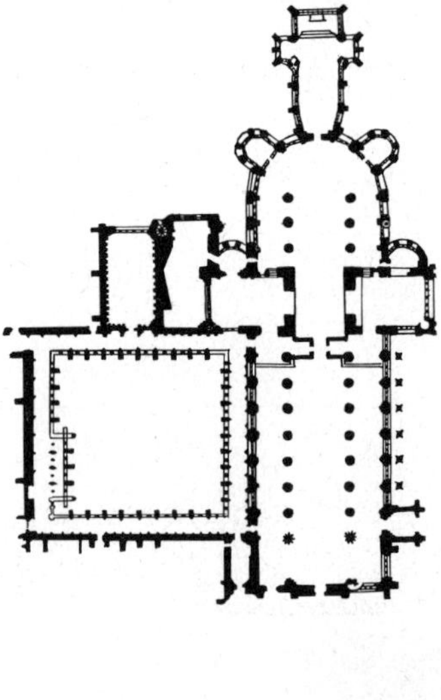

Architecturally the most disparate of the English cathedrals, for the tremendous reconstruction begun in 1331 did not embrace the Norman nave, apart from the two W. bays, rebuilt when the Norman W. towers were removed. This nave, of unusual internal proportions, is ponderous and marred by a too-low 13 c. vault and some dreadful Victorian glass, but is none the less very impressive. The early Perp. choir, with huge windows, has a brittle perfection which is not lovable but leaves one gasping with admiration at its brilliant audacity. Early example of lierne vault, with angel musicians on the bosses over the high altar. Immense E. window with a good deal of its original glass, *c.* 1350. Lady Chapel, virtually independent: a lovely example of Perp., rich and light. Fan-vaulted cloister of great beauty, especially the N. walk, with the monks' *lavatorium*. The sumptuous tower has a grand self-assurance. Much of the close, alas, is now a car park.

Hereford

One of the smaller cathedrals, with an unfortunate architectural history, for the collapse in 1786 of the 14 c. W. tower wrought havoc with the west end, and led to a punitive restoration by Wyatt. But the massive and noble central tower, of *c.*1325, lends distinction to every view of the building; the N. porch, of two dates, is also very handsome. The most interesting feature of the interior is the N. transept, a mannered design of high accomplishment, in which the arches are almost triangular. The Lady Chapel is E.E., with lancet windows set within profusely shafted frames. This interior has greatly benefited from the removal, in 1967, of G. G. Scott's tawdry and inappropriate metal choir screen, but it is still afflicted with some execrable examples of 19 c. glass.

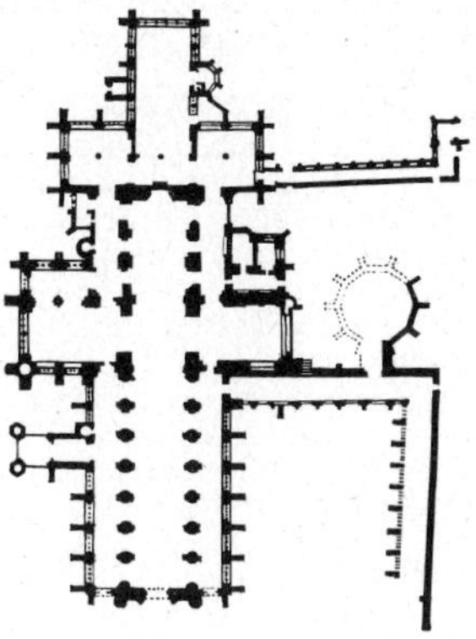

Lichfield

At one time a cathedral of surpassing charm, not all of which has evaporated, despite restorations rendered necessary both by serious damage in the Civil War and by the friability of the local red sandstone. The building is chiefly known for its three stone spires, the Ladies of the Vale, the only English cathedral to have these. Elaborate front with a profusion of platitudinous Victorian sculpture. On the central doors, beautiful scrolled hinges of wrought-iron, the two upper pairs original work of 1293. The interior possesses in full measure the linear richness so characteristic of English Gothic, yet wears an inescapably Victorian air. Fine Lady Chapel, the same height as the choir, but without aisles: the nine very tall windows, suggesting continental inspiration, contain 16 c. Flemish glass. Chapter-house, 1249, an elongated octagon vaulted from a central pier, approached by a vestibule containing a lovely carved arcade.

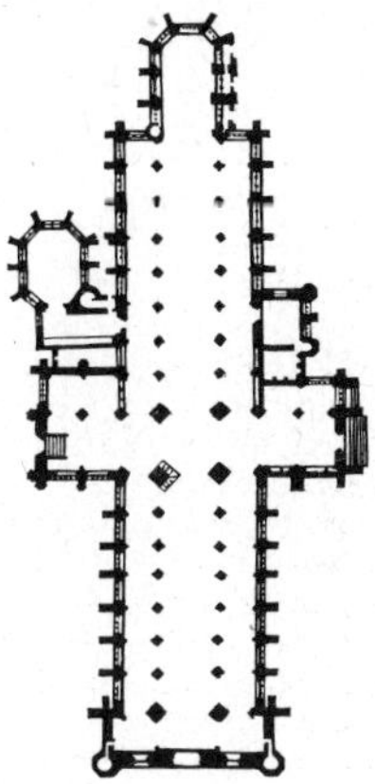

Lincoln

Probably, all things considered, the finest of the English cathedrals. Perched upon a limestone ridge, it is visible in some directions for many miles: the central tower is the loftiest of the English Middle Ages, and one of the most beautiful. The lower parts of the W. towers are Norman, as is the central portion of the W. front, with friezes of sculpture;

but essentially Lincoln is a creation of the 13 c., with 14 c. additions. Specially famous is the Angel Choir of 1256–80, comprising both presbytery and retro-choir. The extraordinary profusion of ornamental carving in stone and wood, together with some fine early glass, means that however much time one is able to spend here, it is never enough. Notable features include the S.E. (or Judgment) porch and the figure a bay to the right of it, often called Margaret of Valois; the pair of stone doorways leading from the great transepts into the N. and S. choir aisles; the exquisitely carved Dec. pulpitum; the choir stalls, of 1360–80, which in the English cathedrals are surpassed only by those of Chester (there are 62 misericords and some very fine stall-ends); carved corbels, head-stops and bosses in all parts of the building but especially in the Angel Choir; early-13 c. stained glass, mutilated but still beautiful, in the four lancets of the S. transept, the rose of the N. transept and the E. windows of the two choir aisles. Fine early-13 c. chapter-house, decagonal, with central pier, marred by poor glass: exquisite capitals in the vestibule. Cloisters with interesting wooden bosses; N. walk, with library over, rebuilt by Wren, 1674.

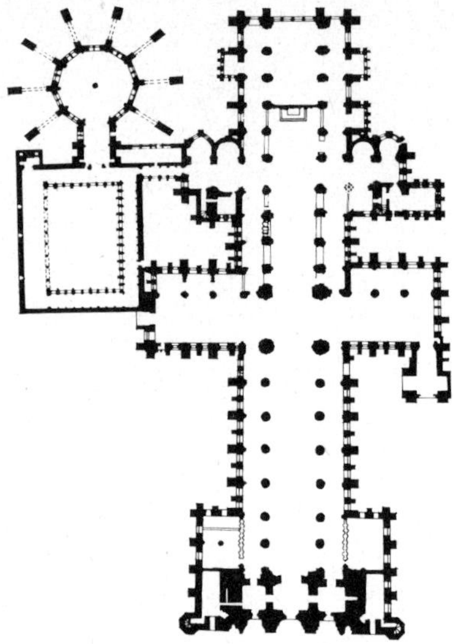

London

St Paul's is England's only major cathedral in the classical style; it was built in 35 years (1675–1710) by a single architect, Christopher Wren, whose masterpiece it is. Larger than any English cathedral of the Middle Ages, even York. Both within and without its dominating feature is the great dome, 102 ft in diameter, one of the finest in the world. This is surmounted by a delightful lantern in tune with the fine pair of Baroque towers at the W. end. The recent cleaning of the white Portland stone (1964–67) has revealed many beautiful carved details by Grinling Gibbons and others long hidden under layers of grime. In plan and to some extent in structure (e.g. in the resort to flying buttresses, hidden behind screen walls) St Paul's owes much to Gothic architecture. Interior: apart from the great central space, the chief pleasures reside in the wood-carving (stalls, organ case, etc.) and in the elaborate wrought-ironwork. Few of the many monuments are works of art.

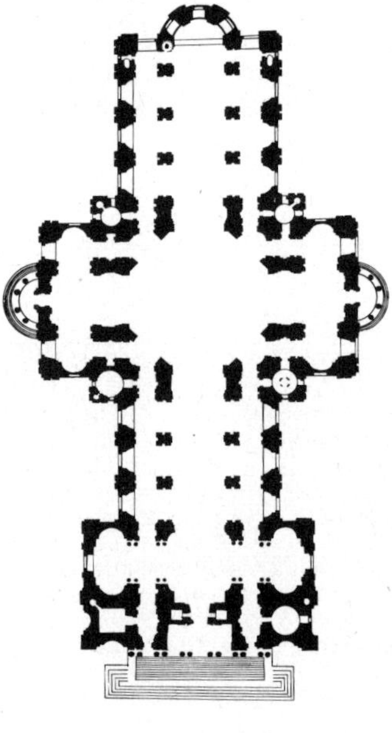

Norwich

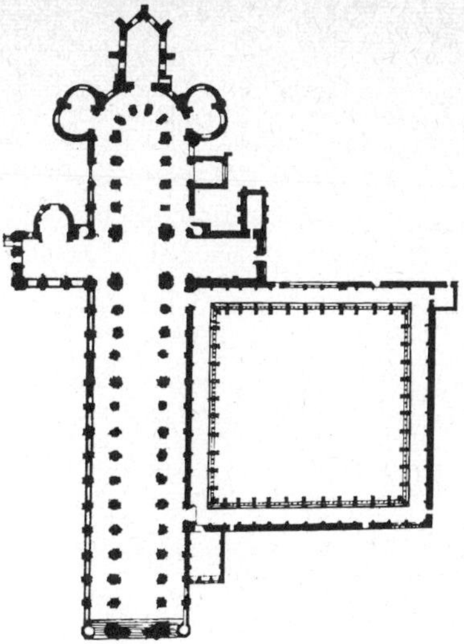

Like Winchester, an amalgam of Romanesque and late-Gothic, and no less successful. The principal pleasures of the exterior are east of the crossing, together with the graceful late-15 c. spire. Within, the Norman work is more in evidence here than at Winchester, but the lovely Perp. lierne vaults extend over nave, transepts and presbytery, to their immense benefit. (All the bosses have been recoloured and regilded.) The nave is 250 ft long: its three eastern bays (of 14) are occupied by the pulpitum and part of the ritual choir, which continues under the crossing. Choir stalls, 15 c., with 62 misericords, a good deal damaged. Splendid presbytery, with apsidal E. end. Prior's door, Dec., opens into large cloisters, gay with re-coloured bosses. Chapter-house destroyed in the reign of Elizabeth I.

Oxford

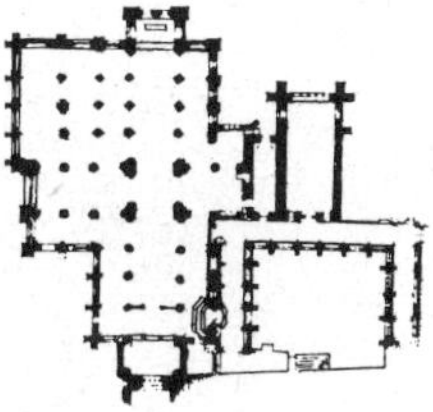

The smallest of the English cathedrals, for this never very large Norman church lost four of the eight bays of its nave when, in 1525, Wolsey laid out the big quadrangle for what was to be his Cardinal College – now the Tom Quad of Christ Church. The exterior is difficult to see; the stone spire, built *c.* 1230 but considerably restored, is among the oldest in the country. The interior has three features of note: the curious double arches of the Norman arcade, presumably a device for suggesting greater height; some attractive 14 c. glass in the S. transept and in the Latin Chapel; and the choir vault. This pendant-lierne vault of the early Tudor period is the special beauty of the only cathedral in the world that serves also as a college chapel.

Peterborough

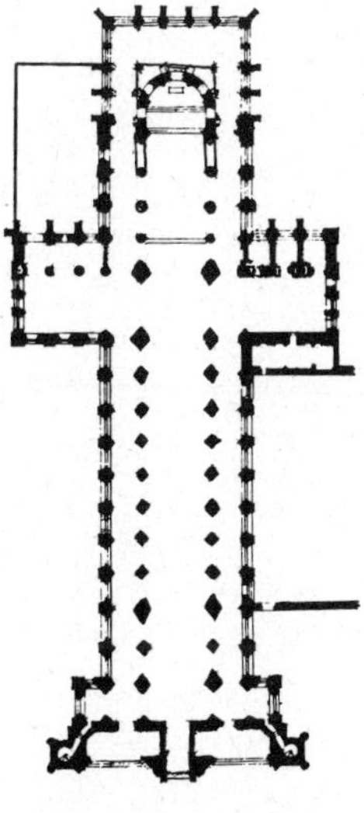

One of the least altered of England's great Norman churches, and after Durham perhaps the finest. The Barnack limestone interior conveys an impression of sober dignity uninterrupted, now, even by a choir screen. The nave has a wooden roof with remarkable paintings originally executed about 1220: in order to see these properly good light and a pair of glasses are essential. The dramatically unexpected W. front is unique in Europe: only the Galilee porch and the pretty little spires are later than 1220. At the other end of the building, a handsome fan-vaulted retro-choir of *c.*1500. The façade apart, the exterior is of much less account than the interior. Only vestiges of the monastic buildings have survived, and even the chapter-house was destroyed after the Dissolution.

Ripon

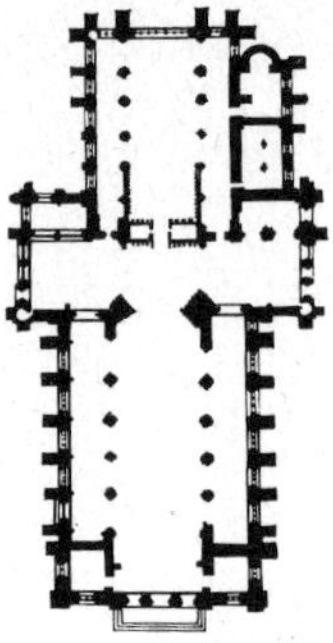

A small cathedral in a mixture of architectural styles, including, for once, Saxon: the Saxon crypt is small and secret. Exterior somewhat dumpy: three towers, all rather squat. The best external features are the W. front, the E. end and the delightful gabled buttresses flanking the nave. Interior short and wide, and unvaulted except in the aisles. The 15 c. pulpitum, with organ loft completely blocking the view of the choir, is unwelcome here. Sedilia rich Dec. Choir stalls (1490) fine though much restored, with 34 misericords: a notable set, with many animals.

Rochester

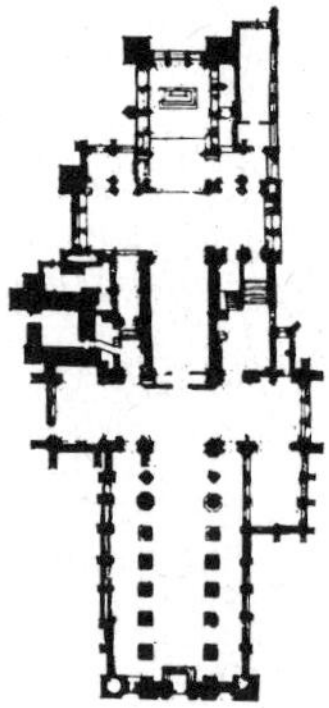

A comparatively small building greatly altered and reconstructed. Basically the façade and nave are Norman and the rest E.E. The only notable feature of the exterior is the damaged 12 c. W. door, showing marked French influence. Interior: pleasing Norman nave; raised choir with crypt under, as at Canterbury, but here the crypt has no sculptural interest. Fine mid-14 c. doorway leading from S.E. transept to what is now the chapter-room. The former chapter-house and other monastic buildings have all perished.

St Albans

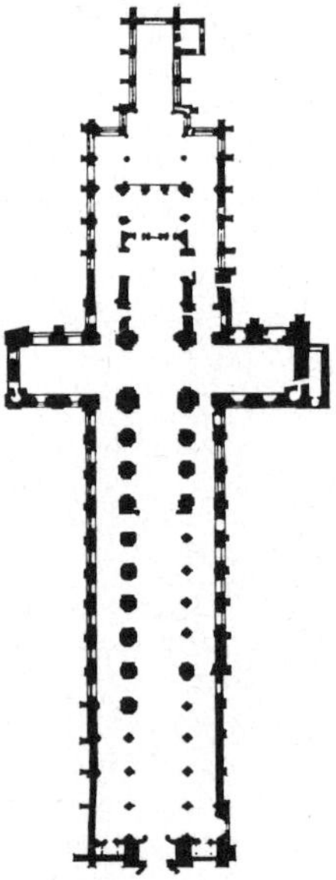

Longer than any other English cathedral except Winchester, this once famous abbey church fell for want of funds into a shocking state of disrepair in the 18 c. and early 19 c., and has undergone very drastic restoration. Apart from the early Norman tower, largely built of Roman bricks, there is now little to be enjoyed outside, but the interior is still imposing, especially at the crossing, with its grand Norman arches. Notable features include, in the nave, remains of wall-paintings – a series of Crucifixions – of 13 c. and 14 c., and the only stone rood screen in an English cathedral; over the choir and presbytery, painted wooden roofs, the latter (late 13 c.) in the form of a ribbed vault; and a lofty reredos of 1484, with Victorian figures, behind which, in the chapel of St Alban, is an oak watching-loft of *c.*1400.

Salisbury

Stately and aloof, this cathedral, all erected between 1220 and 1380, is a key building for an understanding of English architecture. Exterior dominated by the incomparable spire, the loftiest stone spire of the Middle Ages (404 ft), rising above a very fine Dec. tower. The rest mostly E.E., very precisely detailed, and with a profusion of lancet windows. Interior also distinguished by purity of detail, and by abundant use of dark Purbeck marble to contrast with the light Chilmark limestone; very little sculpture, and now not much glass either. Choir greatly improved in 1959–60 by the removal of wretched Victorian furnishings: fussy brass screen, altar rails, reredos, glazed tile floor, etc. Front of original stone pulpitum, with excellent figure carvings, still preserved in N.E. transept. Very fine early-Dec. cloisters, the largest in England. Octagonal chapter-house with central pier, copied from Westminster: still badly in need of de-Victorianising. The late-18 c. close, with its acres of lawn always faultlessly mown, provides the perfect setting.

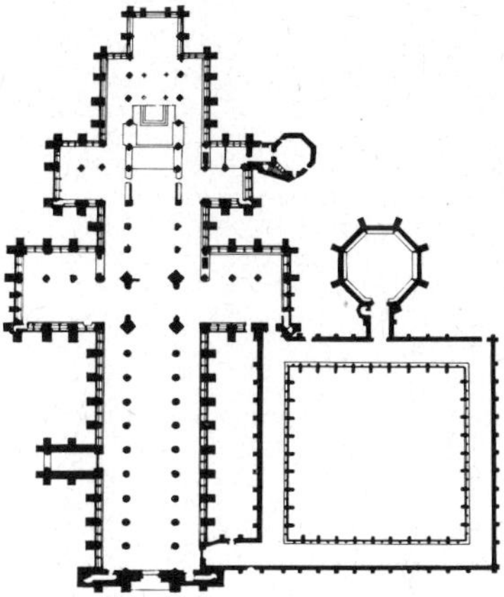

Southwark

As at Bristol, the eastern half of the cathedral alone is medieval: the old nave survived until the 1830s, when it was declared unsafe. The present nave dates only from 1889–97. And even the eastern arm is incomplete, as the Lady Chapel was lopped off for road-widening. Very unlucky in its site, the exterior is no longer enjoyable; but within, the choir, of modest dimensions, is a good example of E.E. at its purest. Behind the lofty Tudor reredos (with statues all renewed) stretches the low rectangular E.E. retro-choir, four bays by three, with pleasing cross-vistas.

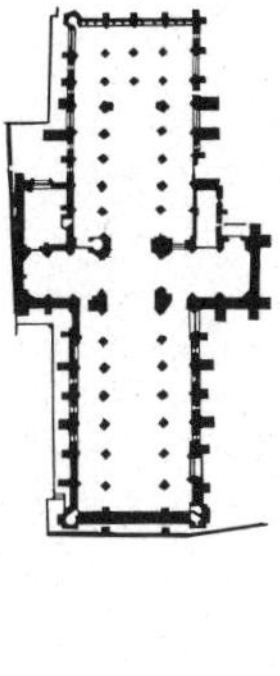

Southwell

England's smallest cathedral city, pronounced Suth'll ('th' as in 'the'), has a cathedral which is also on the small side, but full of pleasures. Exterior long and low and all the elevations excessively flat; the appeal is principally internal. The unvaulted Norman nave, with unusual 'port-hole' windows in the clere-story, has a simple dignity and the arches at the crossing are lofty and strong. But the Gothic portions are the best. E.E. choir: small but very pleasing. Dec. pulpitum sumptuous, especially on the E. side. The organ fills the arch above and so cuts off the choir completely from the rest of the church: a bad arrangement. Six canopied stalls with fine misericords. The small octagonal chapter-house and its vestibule constitute the supreme example of middle-Gothic nature-worship. The Leaves of Southwell are deservedly famous.

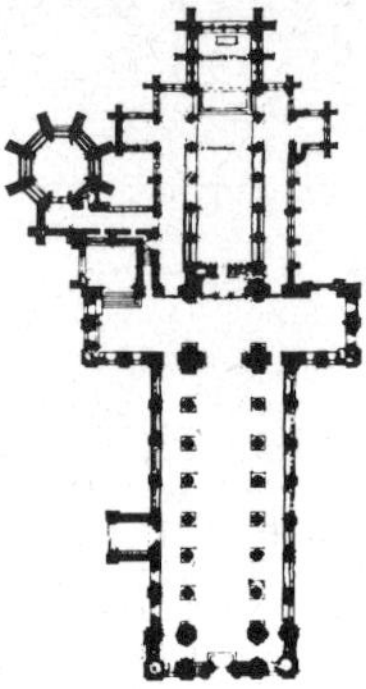

Wells

A queen among cathedrals: graceful, subtle, marvellously embellished with sculptured details and in its eastern part a jewel-box of sparkling glass – yellow, brown, ruby, olive green, white: and hardly any blue. The most poetic of the English cathedrals, marred only by the obtrusive 'scissor' arches inserted in 14 c. with great ingenuity to support the weight of the central tower. The W. front, with far more original sculpture than any other, is beyond doubt the finest in the country, as also is the exquisite, elevated, octagonal chapter-house. N. porch, *c.*1215, a work of grave beauty. The central tower outstanding even in Somerset, a county famed for the splendour of its church towers. Special delights of the interior: E.E. arcade of nave and transepts, with stiff-leaf capitals which embrace figure-carving; vault under tower; set of 60 misericords of *c.*1330 which are among the finest in England; late-Dec. stone-panelled presbytery with the Golden Window; retro-choir with fascinating cross-vistas; Lady Chapel with its rich glass and star-vault. Good 15 c. cloisters. Wells has a specially attractive setting: to W. a broad green close; to S. the moated Bishop's Palace (13–14 c.); to N. the Vicars' Close, a completely preserved mediaeval street; and to N.E. Mendip hills.

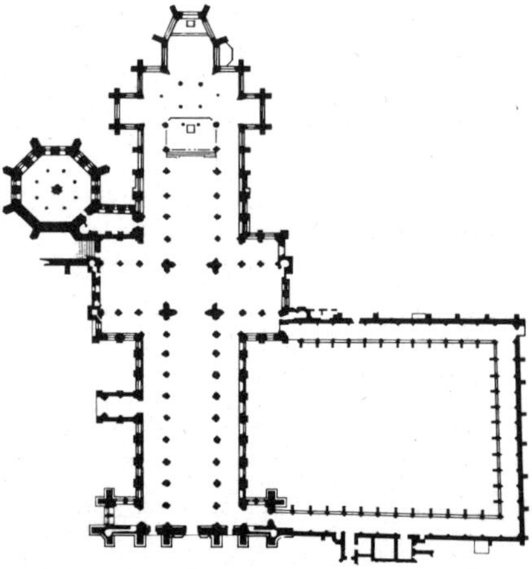

Winchester

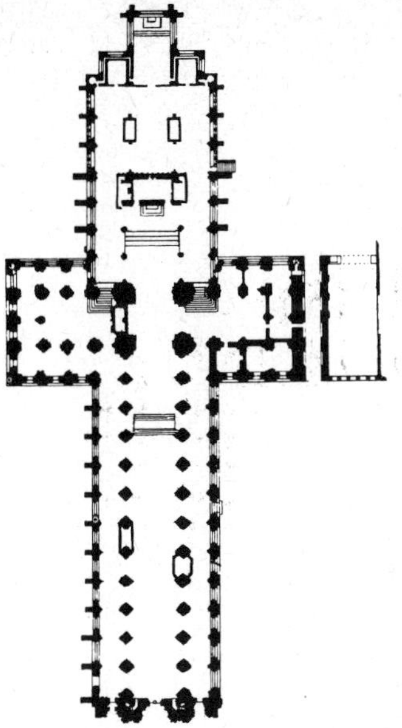

The longest Gothic church in Europe: 556 ft. Externally disappointing, but the interior is not only magnificent in its general aspect but packed with interest. The nave, an ingenious combination of Norman and Perp., is superb. The transepts, with flat wooden roofs, show better than anywhere else the bold scale and stark unadorned vigour of early Norman church-building. The eastern arm is the most elegant part of the cathedral although the early-16c. vault is only a wooden imitation of stone. Behind the lofty Perp. reredos are the E.E. retro-choir and the Lady Chapel, the latter much darkened by poor Victorian glass. Very little medieval glass remains, but elsewhere the Victorian glass is better. Three sets of medieval paintings, of which those in the Chapel of the Holy Sepulchre of *c.*1225, entered from the N. transept (by application to a verger), are of exceptional quality for England. Font, *c.*1180, of black Tournai marble. Virgin and Child, stone, *c.*1340, in the choir: a precious fragment. Notable stalls of *c.*1320, with 60 small but vigorous misericords. Retro-choir has the most extensive medieval tiled floor in the country. Numerous tombs, several in chantry chapels, of which that of William of Wykeham in the nave, to whom the fabric owes so much, is appropriately the finest.

Worcester

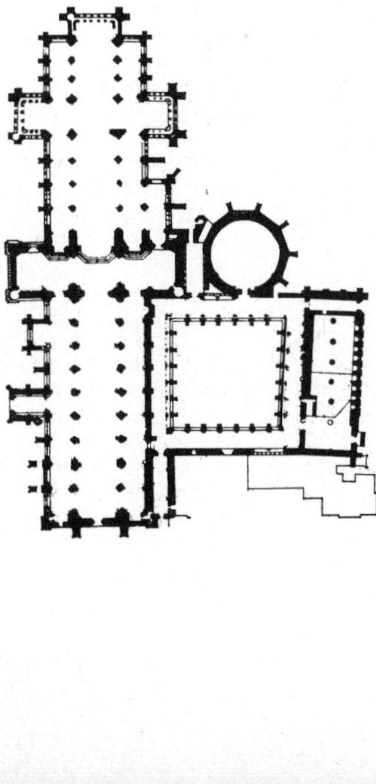

A cathedral with important parts in every style from early Norman to Perp. Norman: the dark, many-aisled crypt and the striking chapter-house, circular within, decagonal without since *c.*1400 when the walls were strengthened. Transitional: the two strange W. bays of the nave. E.E.: the choir and lofty retro-choir, the finest portion of the building. Dec. and Perp.: seven bays of the nave, the N. porch, cloisters and handsome central tower. The vigorously carved misericords, dating from 1379, include a complete set of Occupations of the Months. Worcester is a building of potential distinction, at present seriously compromised internally by unworthy Victorian fittings which go far towards spoiling one's pleasure. Outside, drastic refacing following upon the decay of the soft local sandstone has deprived the cathedral of all its texture. It is therefore seen to best advantage from across the Severn.

York

The largest of England's medieval cathedrals; and although without the charm of some of the others its scale never fails to impress. All three phases of English Gothic are prominent: E.E. in the transepts; Dec. in the nave, W. front and chapter-house; Perp. in the choir and big central tower. W. front rich and intricate; N. front, with the Five Sisters windows, a memorable example of the lancet style at its most austere. Interior broad and lofty, yet lacking in magic: unfortunately none of the main vaults is of stone. Pulpitum late-15c. York is famous for its stained glass; none of it is of the very highest quality, but there is far more mediaeval glass here than in any other English church, and its marked superiority to nearly all Victorian and more recent glass will be apparent at once. The beautiful octagonal chapter-house (with no central pier, as the roof is again of wood) has fine naturalistic carving.

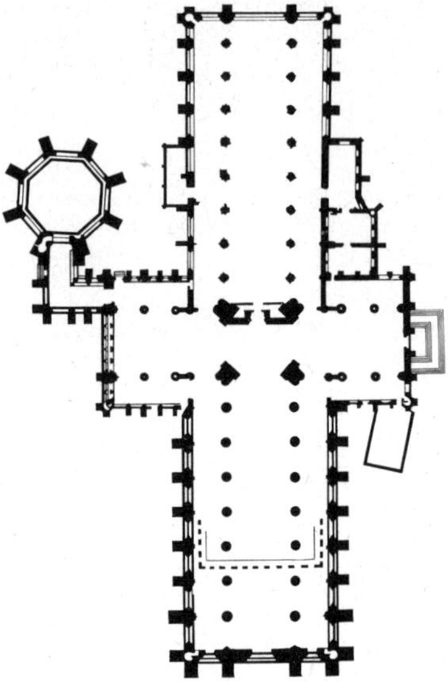

Acknowledgements

MARTIN HÜRLIMANN: 2, 3, 6, 9, 14, 15, 17, 20, 21, 22, Plate II, 24, 25, 26, 28, 30, 32, 33, 34, 35, 36, 44, Plate III, Plate IV, 46, 47, 51, 54, 55, 56, 57, 59, 60, 62, 63, 64, 68, 71, 75, 81, 83, 84, 85, 86, 91, 92, 94, 96, 98, 110, 111, 114, 116, 117, 118, 119, 121, 123, 124, 126, 127, 130, 134, 135, 137, 138, 139, 142, 143, 146, 151, 153, 154, 167, 168, 169, 171, 172, 173, 175, 178, 180, 181, 182, 185, 186, 187, 189, 196, 197, 198, 199.
Aerofilms: 43, 58, 108, 115, 145, 161.
A.F. Kersting: Plate I.
John Champion Ltd, Salisbury: 69.
NATIONAL MONUMENTS' RECORD: 31, 40, 61, 70, 77, 78, 99, 140, 163, 183, Mrs Brocklesby: 66, Stewart Bull Ltd: 192, C.J.P. Cave: 38, 39, 106, F.H. Crossley: 5, 76, 102, 104, 113, 136, H. Felton: 7, 11, 12, 23, 41, 42, 48, 49, 50, 52, 53, 67, 72, 74, 80, 82, 87, 90, 95, 103, 105, 107, 112, 120, 122, 125, 144, 150, 162, 164, 177, 179, 184, Fox Photos: 155, H. Gernsheim: 188, S.O. Gorse: 148, E.H. Grice: 174, A.F. Kersting: 65, G.B. Mason: 13, F.L. Palmer: 27, 170, S. Pitcher: 10, 19, 144, 165, W. Scott: 18, 29, 37, 45, 109, 128, 129, 156, 158, 160, E. Shirley-Jones: 100, 152, S. Smith: 8, 88, 89, 93, 131, 132, V. Turl: 147, Dr Weaver: 157, 176, R.F. Willis: 166.

Glossary of Architectural Terms

ABUTMENT: A pier or wall of solid masonry erected to counter the thrust of an arch or vault.

AMBULATORY: A processional aisle encircling, at a lower level, an apse.

ANNULET: A ring round a circular pier or shaft.

APSE: A semicircular or polygonal end to a church or chapel, usually vaulted.

ARCADE: A range of arches resting on piers or columns. A 'blind arcade' is an arcade attached to a wall.

ARMATURE: A metal framework, in the Middle Ages always of iron, introduced into a large untraceried window to support the stained glass. Armatures were sometimes wrought into elaborate decorative patterns.

BALL-FLOWER: A form of ornament consisting of globular three-petalled flowers enclosing small balls; characteristic of the Decorated period.

BOSS: In ribbed vaulting, an ornamental projection, generally carved with foliage or figures, used to conceal the intersection of the ribs.

CHANTRY CHAPEL: A small chapel within a cathedral or other church, endowed for the saying of Masses for the soul of the donor.

CHAPTER HOUSE: The administrative office of a foundation.

CHEVET: French term for an east end when it comprises an apse, ambulatory and radiating chapels.

CHEVRON: A zigzag form of ornamentation characteristic of the Norman period.

CHOIR: In the exact sense, that part of the cathedral, east of the screen or pulpitum and west of the presbytery, in which the service is sung. In architecture the term is sometimes loosely applied to the whole eastern arm; on the other hand, the ritual choir may be partly located under the crossing and may even extend into the architectural nave.

CINQUEFOIL: A five-lobed ornamental infilling for a circle or archhead.

CLERESTORY: The upper part of the nave, choir and transepts, containing a series of windows clear of the roofs of the aisles.

CORBEL: A block of stone projecting from a wall in support of a roof, vault, parapet, shaft or other feature. Corbels were often adorned with carving.

CROCKETS: In Gothic architecture, ornaments, usually in the form of buds or curled leaves, placed at regular intervals on the sloping sides of spires, gables, canopies, pinnacles, etc.

CUSPS: In Gothic arches or tracery, the projecting points between the lobes or foils.

DIAPER: An all-over pattern of squares or diamonds, incised or in low relief, covering a plain wall-surface.

DOG-TOOTH: A form of ornament consisting of a succession of raised tooth-like pieces, arranged in pairs or groups of four, and set diagonally to each other, usually in a hollow moulding; characteristic of the Early English period.

ENGAGED SHAFT or COLUMN: A shaft or column partly let into a wall, a pier, or a larger shaft or column.

FAN VAULT: A conoidal type of vault in which the length and curvature of all the ribs (which are decorative and not structural) is similar; confined to the Perpendicular period.

GALILEE: A term sometimes applied in France to a narthex or entrance vestibule, but in England (cf. Ely and Lincoln) to a large porch, included in the route of the Sunday procession: the symbolical reference was to Christ going before his disciples into Galilee after the Resurrection (cf. Matthew, ch. 28, v.10; Mark, ch. 16, v.7). At Durham, exceptionally, the Galilee was a Lady Chapel (see p. 48).

GARTH: The area enclosed by cloisters.

GRISAILLE: Greyish-white glass, ornamented with monochrome decoration in neutral-coloured enamel used like paint and fired into the glass.

GROINED VAULT: A vault resulting from the intersection at right angles of two tunnel vaults; no ribs.

HALL-CHURCH: A church in which the aisles are of the same height as the rest.

HAMMER-BEAMS: Beams projecting at right angles, generally from the top of a wall, to provide support for the vertical members and/or arched braces of a wooden roof.

LADY CHAPEL: A chapel dedicated to the Virgin, usually situated at the east end.

LANCET WINDOW: A narrow window terminating in a sharp point; characteristic of the Early English period.

LANTERN TOWER: A tower in which the crossing space is extended upwards and lit from the upper windows.

LIERNE RIBS: Short subsidiary vaulting ribs serving a purely decorative purpose: characteristic of the later Decorated and Perpendicular periods.

LIERNE VAULT: A vault incorporating such ribs.

MINSTER: A term indicative of a large church but, surprisingly, with no precise signification. Apart from West Minster—i.e. the minster west of the city of London—this lovely title is invariably applied to only three English churches: York, Beverley and Wimborne, of which the first alone is a cathedral. Of the other cathedrals, Ripon is called 'the Minster' frequently; Lincoln and Southwell sometimes; Lichfield now very seldom.

MISERICORD: A bracket on the underside of a hinged wooden seat in a choir stall, which, when turned up, afforded support during long periods of standing, and is often found to be enriched with lively carvings. Sometimes called a MISERERE.

MOULDINGS: The varieties of contour given to piers, arches, etc., in order to obtain effects of richness through light and shade contrasts.

MULLION: A vertical structural member subdividing a window.

NARTHEX: A covered vestibule or porch stretching across the western end of many large churches; only found on the Continent.

NAVE: The western arm of a church, eastwards from the inner door.

OGEE: A continuous double curve, concave above and convex below, or vice versa: specially characteristic of the later Decorated period.

PIER: A solid masonry support designed to sustain vertical pressure. Piers may be simple (round, square, rectangular) or compound, composite, multiform—i.e. of more complex profile, achieved by applying mouldings, engaged shafts, etc.

PRESBYTERY (or SANCTUARY): The part of a major church, east of the choir, in which the high altar is situated.

PULPITUM: The solid screen shutting off the ritual choir from the nave in a major church and providing, on its eastern side, a backing for the return stalls (see pp. 21–22). Originally the word signified the platform or gallery on top of the screen.

QUADRIPARTITE VAULT: A vault divided by transverse, diagonal and wall ribs into four compartments of equal size.

QUATREFOIL: A four-lobed ornamental infilling for a circle or arch-head.

RETICULATED TRACERY: Tracery in which a single pattern, consisting of circles drawn out at top and bottom into ogee-shaped points, is repeated over a whole area.

RETRO-CHOIR: The part of a major church which lies beyond the presbytery, i.e. east of the high altar (but not including the Lady Chapel).

RIBS: See LIERNE RIBS, RIDGE RIB, TIERCERON RIBS.

RIDGE RIB: The moulded rib running along the apex of a vault.

RITUAL CHOIR: See CHOIR.

ROOD SCREEN: A screen, placed originally one bay west of the pulpitum, and usually of wood, with a coved loft for supporting the rood (see p. 21).

SANCTUARY: Synonymous with PRESBYTERY, *q.v.*

SEXPARTITE VAULT: A quadripartite vault (*q.v.*) into which an additional transverse rib has been introduced, thus dividing it into six compartments (of unequal size) instead of four.

SHAFT-RING: See ANNULET.

SPANDREL: The space, approximately triangular, between the outer curve of an arch and the rectangle formed by the mouldings enclosing it; or the space between the shoulders of two contiguous arches and the moulding or string-course above them.

SPIRE LIGHT (or LUCARNE): A vertical opening in the tapering surface of a spire, gabled and usually traceried but never glazed.

STIFF-LEAF: The foliage of conventional form, with stiff stems and lobed leaves, that characterizes Early English ornament on mouldings, capitals, corbels, bosses, etc.

STRING-COURSE: A moulding or narrow projecting course running horizontally along the face of a wall.

TIERCERON RIBS: Pairs of ribs with the same point of springing as the principal ribs but which meet obliquely instead of being carried across from one side of a vault to the other in a continuous line (see pp. 90–91).

TIERCERON VAULT: A vault incorporating such ribs.

TRACERY: The intersecting ornamental ribwork in the upper parts of Gothic windows; also on walls, screens, vaults, etc. The earliest form, Plate tracery, in which decoratively shaped openings appear to be cut out of infillings of solid stone, soon (*c.* 1250) gave place to Bar tracery, in which the mullions are continued upwards to produce patterns of various kinds.

TRANSEPT: An arm of the cross-piece of a cruciform church.

TRANSOM: A horizontal structural member subdividing a window.

TRANSVERSE: A term applied to vault-ribs or arches set at right angles to the axis of the portion of the building in question.

TREFOIL: A three-lobed or trifoliate ornamental infilling for a circle or arch-head.

TRIBUNE: A gallery extending over the whole roof—usually a stone vault—of an aisle (see p. 32).

TRIFORIUM: An arcaded wall passage or area of blank arcading above the main arcade of a church and below the clerestory. In smaller churches and in some large ones of late-Gothic date the triforium stage was omitted. The extension of this term to include galleries is still followed by some writers but is not recommended. (See TRIBUNE).

TYMPANUM (plural: TYMPANA): The area between the lintel and the arch of a doorway, often filled with relief sculpture.

VAULTING: See FAN VAULT, GROINED VAULT, LIERNE VAULT, QUADRIPARTITE VAULT, SEXPARTITE VAULT, TIERCERON VAULT.

VESICA: A pointed oval, composed of the segments of two intersecting circles of equal diameter.

VOUSSOIR: A wedge-shaped stone for an arch.

WAGON ROOF: A curved wooden rafter roof, recalling, inside, the canvas tilt or awning over an old-fashioned wagon.

Index

The more important references are indicated in **bold** type.
The illustrations, which have their own series of numbers, are indicated in *italics*.